The Other Book

Also by Mitchell Symons

Nonfiction

That Book . . . of Perfectly Useless Information

This Book . . . of More Perfectly Useless Information

Why Girls Can't Throw . . . and Other Questions
You Always Wanted Answered

Forfeit!

The Equation Book of Sports Crosswords

The Equation Book of Movie Crosswords

The "You" Magazine Book of Journolists (four books; coauthor)

Movielists (coauthor)

The "Sunday" Magazine Book of Crosswords

The "Hello!" Magazine Book of Crosswords (three books)

How to Be Fat: The Chip and Fry Diet (coauthor)

The Book of Criminal Records

The Book of Lists

The Book of Celebrity Lists

The Book of Celebrity Sex Lists

The Bill Clinton Joke Book

National Lottery Big Draw 2000 (coauthor)

Fiction

All In

The Lot

The Other Book

...OF THE MOST PERFECTLY USELESS INFORMATION

Mitchell Symons

HarperEntertainment

An Imprint of HarperCollins*Publishers*

HarperCollins books may be purchased for educational, business, or sales
promotional use. For information please write: Special Markets
Department, HarperCollins Publishers, 10 East 53rd Street, New York,
NY 10022.

FIRST EDITION

Designed by Chris Welch

Library of Congress Cataloging-in-Publication Data

Symons, Mitchell.
    The other book — of the most perfectly useless information /
by Mitchell Symons.
        p. cm.
    Includes index.
    ISBN-13: 978-0-06-113405-0
    ISBN-10: 0-06-113405-8
  1. Handbooks, vade-mecums, etc. I. Title.

AG106.S94 2006
031.02—dc22   2006043364

06 07 08 09 10 ❖/RRD 10 9 8 7 6 5 4 3 2 1

To Penny, Jack and Charlie
with all my love

More appealing than knowledge itself
is the feeling of knowledge.
—DANIEL J. BOORSTIN

The Other Book

Firsts

Orville Wright was involved in the **first aircraft accident** (his passenger was killed).

Thomas Jefferson grew the **first tomatoes** in the United States. He wanted to prove to Americans that they were not poisonous (which people believed them to be).

The **first female host** of *Saturday Night Live* was Candice Bergen.

The **first photograph of the moon** was taken in 1839 by Louis Daguerre, but the details were indiscernible. J. W. Draper took the **first** recognizable photograph in 1840.

Legend has it that the **first electric Christmas lights** were put together by a telephone switchboard installer. Candles were deemed to be too dangerous near a telephone switchboard, so the installer took some lights from an old switchboard, connected them together, hooked them up to a battery and put them around a Christmas tree.

The **first process of color photography**—using three colors—was patented (by William Morgan-Brown) in 1876.

Sunglasses first became popular in the 1920s, when movie stars began wearing them to counteract the photographers' bright lights.

Pickled herrings were **first eaten** in the fourteenth century.

Jim Morrison of the Doors was the **first rock star** to be arrested onstage.

The world's **first cash dispenser** was opened by British actor Reg Varney at Barclays Bank, Enfield, London, in 1967.

The **first heart pacemaker** (external) was fitted in 1952. The **first *internal* pacemaker** was fitted in 1958. The **first successful heart operation** had been carried out in 1896 by Louis Rehn in Frankfurt, Germany.

The **duplicating machine** was **first patented by James Watt** in 1780. The photocopier was invented in 1938 by Chester Carlson of New York.

Linoleum, the floor covering used in many kitchens, was **first patented** in 1863 by Frederick Walton of London.

The London Underground system was **first used** in 1863.

The typewriter was **first patented** by Henry Mill in 1714, but he never managed to market his invention.

The **first toothbrush** was invented in China in 1498.

In 1840, **Henry Wadsworth Longfellow** became the first **American** to have plumbing installed in his house.

The **first word spoken** by an ape in the movie *Planet of the Apes* was "Smile."

Ties were first worn in Croatia (which is why they were called cravats, originally *à la croate*).

The **first phone directory** in the United States was published by the New Haven District Telephone Company in Connecticut in 1878. It had only 50 names. The **first British telephone directory** was published by the London Telephone Company in 1880. It listed in excess of 250 names and numbers.

The **first electric burglar alarm** was installed in 1858 by one Edwin T. Holmes of Boston, Massachusetts. It is not recorded whether or not the alarm worked.

Marilyn Monroe's first modeling agency had offices in the Ambassador Hotel—the same hotel in which Robert F. Kennedy was assassinated.

The **first commercially successful escalator** was patented in 1892 by Jesse Reno of New York.

The **first police force** was established in Paris in 1667.

The **first taxis** with metered fares were operational in 1907.

The **first British Christmas card** showed people drinking, and so the temperance societies tried to get it banned.

The **first Harley-Davidson motorcycle** was built in 1903 and used a tomato can as a carburetor.

Mark Knopfler wrote the **first-ever CD single** ("Brothers in Arms").

The **first fax machine** was patented in 1843, thirty-three years before Alexander Graham Bell demonstrated the telephone.

The **first organized Christmas Day swim** in the freezing-cold Serpentine in London's Hyde Park took place in 1864.

The **first episode** of *Joanie Loves Chachi* was the highest-rated American program in the history of Korean television. *Chachi* is Korean for "penis."

Pitcairn Airlines was the **first airline** to provide airsick bags (in 1922).

The **first-ever Royal Christmas broadcast** was made by King George V on radio in 1932.

The **first contraceptive** was crocodile dung, used by Egyptians in 2000 B.C.

The **first song to be performed in outer space** was "Happy Birthday"—sung by the *Apollo 9* astronauts on March 8, 1969.

In 1933, on his thirty-second birthday, **Rudy Vallee** became the **first person** to receive a singing telegram.

The **first personal computer,** the Apple II, went on sale in 1977 (its hard drive had a capacity of just five megabytes).

Wrigley's first chewing gum was called "Vassar" (after the college).

The U.K. boasts the world's **first speed limit.** It was established in 1865 and was set at 2 miles per hour. In 1903, the year the driver's license was introduced, it was raised to 20 miles per hour.

Burt Bacharach's first professional job was as an accompanist to Vic Damone.

The **first credit card** was Diners Club (in 1950). There were just two hundred card holders.

Popcorn was on the menu at the **first Thanksgiving dinner.**

When the **first ballpoint pen** was sold in New York (on October 9, 1945), it was priced at $12.50, and yet more than five thousand people crashed the gates at Gimbel's to buy one.

The **first domain name** to be registered was Symbolics.com (in March 1985).

The **first man-made object** to break the sound barrier was a whip.

In 1894, **boxing** became the **first sport** to be filmed.

Benjamin Franklin was America's **first newspaper cartoonist.**

Glenn Miller was the **first artist** to receive a gold record (for "Chattanooga Choo Choo" in 1942).

In 1954, Richard Herrick received the **first successful kidney transplant** (it was donated by his twin brother, Ronald).

The **first motel**—The Motel Inn—opened in 1925 in San Luis Obispo, California.

The **first CD** released in the United States was Bruce Springsteen's *Born in the USA.*

In 1915, *Birth of a Nation* became the **first movie** to be shown at the White House.

People Born on Significant Days in History

Michael Imperioli—the day Colonel Jean-Bédel Bokassa took over the Central African Republic after a coup (January 1, 1966)

Nicolas Cage—the day the British Leyland Motor Company challenged the U.S. blockade by selling 450 buses to Cuba (January 7, 1964)

Steven Soderbergh—the day George Wallace became governor of Alabama (January 14, 1963)

Aaliyah—the day the shah of Iran fled the country (January 16, 1979)

Bridget Fonda—the day France and China announced their decision to establish diplomatic relations (January 27, 1964)

Dr. Dre—the day Gambia gained independence from the U.K. (February 18, 1965)

Queen Latifah—the day Prince Sihanouk of Cambodia was deposed (March 18, 1970)

Sarah Jessica Parker—the day Martin Luther King Jr. led civil-rights activists on a march from Selma to Montgomery (March 25, 1965)

Uma Thurman—the day the United States invaded Cambodia (April 29, 1970)

Mike Myers—the day the Organization of African Unity was established (May 25, 1963)

Heidi Klum—the day the Greek military junta overthrew the monarchy and proclaimed a republic (June 1, 1973)

Anna Kournikova—the day Israel destroyed Iraq's nuclear reactor (June 7, 1981)

Elizabeth Hurley—the day of the Battle of Dong Xoai in the Vietnam War (June 10, 1965)

Joanne Harris—the day that President Johnson signed the Civil Rights Act into law (July 3, 1964)

Lleyton Hewitt—the day that Jean Harris was convicted of murdering Dr. Herman Tarnower, creator of the Scarsdale Diet (February 24, 1981)

Christian Slater—the final day of Woodstock (August 18, 1969)

Maria von Trapp—the day the Cullinan Diamond was found (January 26, 1905)

John Grisham—the day Georgy Malenkov resigned as premier of the Soviet Union (February 8, 1955)

Kiri Te Kanawa—the day the U.S. Air Force began daylight bombing raids on Berlin (March 6, 1944)

Ken Norton—the day the atomic bomb was dropped on Nagasaki (August 8, 1945)

José Feliciano—the day Vidkun Quisling was sentenced to death for treason (September 10, 1945)

Elie Wiesel—the day the discovery of penicillin was announced (September 30, 1928)

Spiro Agnew—the day the kaiser abdicated (November 9, 1918)

Calvin Klein—the day the Russians counterattacked at Stalingrad (November 19, 1942)

Joe Walsh—the day Princess (now Queen) Elizabeth married Prince Philip (November 20, 1947)

Jimi Hendrix—the day the French fleet was sunk at Toulon (November 27, 1942)

Randy Newman—the day the Tehran Conference took place (November 28, 1943)

People Who Were Born/ Grew Up in Poverty

Clara Bow, Kenneth Branagh, Robert Burns, Michael Caine, Mariah Carey, Miguel de Cervantes, Coco Chanel, Ray Charles, Arthur Conan Doyle, Billy Connolly, Joan Crawford, Kirk Douglas, Cary Grant, Susan Hayward, Harry Houdini, Jesse Jackson, Nikita Khrushchev, Lennox Lewis, Sonny Liston, Harold Lloyd, Sophia Loren, John Lydon, Johnny Rotten, Anna Magnani, Diego Maradona, Walter Matthau, Marilyn Monroe, V. S. Naipaul, Dolly Parton, Pelé, Sidney Poitier, Elvis Presley, Rene Russo, Gerhard Schröder, Maria Sharapova, Hilary Swank, Billy Bob Thornton, Mao Tse-tung, Shania Twain, Pancho Villa, Oprah Winfrey

Pure Trivia

Diet Coke was invented in 1982. However, in 1379 a Mr. and Mrs. Coke of Yorkshire, England, named their daughter Diot (a diminutive of Dionisia, the modern-day name Denise).

More than half the world's people have never made or received a telephone call.

The buzz generated by an electric razor in Britain is in the key of G. In America it is in the key of B-flat.

Henry Ford never had a driver's license.

Popeye's friend Wimpy's full name is J. Wellington Wimpy.

Popeye's girlfriend, Olive, had a brother called Castor Oyl.

According to Beatles producer George Martin, the 1960s *Batman* theme song inspired George Harrison to write the hit song "Taxman."

Ketchup was once sold as a medicine.

In 1961 the Museum of Modern Art in New York City hung Henri Matisse's painting *Le Bateau* upside down for forty-seven days before an art student noticed the error.

The original name of Pac-Man was going to be Puck-Man, until executives saw the obvious potential for parody.

In a poll, 97 percent of Canadians said they would not borrow a toothbrush if they forgot to pack their own.

The song "When Irish Eyes Are Smiling" was written by a German, George Graff, who never once visited Ireland.

Good Friday once fell on Boxing Day. (It was a horse named Good Friday, and it fell in a race on December 26, 1899.)

The Snickers bar was named after a horse the Mars family owned.

L. Frank Baum got the name Oz in *The Wizard of Oz* from one of his alphabetized filing cabinets (O–Z).

Al Capone's older brother was a policeman in Nebraska.

The Lone Ranger's real name was John Reid.

Humans have 46 chromosomes, peas have 14, and crayfish have 200.

Walter Raleigh's black greyhound was named Hamlet.

In ancient China people committed suicide by eating a pound of salt.

The straw was invented by Egyptian brewers in order to taste beer during brewing without disturbing the fermenting matter floating on the top.

Cabbage is 91 percent water.

There is enough lead in the average pencil to draw a line 35 miles long.

Walt Disney named Mickey Mouse after Mickey Rooney, whose mother he dated. (N.B.: Walt Disney was afraid of mice.)

Coca-Cola has a pH of 2.5.

Five percent of Canadians don't know the first 7 words of the Canadian anthem, but know the first 9 of the American anthem.

Sixty-five percent of Elvis impersonators are of Asian descent.

Donald Duck has a sister called Dumbella.

Siamese twins Chang and Eng Bunker once beat each other up over alcohol.

Oscars given out during World War II were made of plaster because metal was in short supply.

In 1920, 57 percent of Hollywood movies billed the female star above the leading man. In 1990, only 18 percent had the leading lady given top billing.

Buenos Aires has more psychoanalysts per head than any other place in the world.

There are three Gershwin songs — "Nice Work If You Can Get It," "I Got Rhythm" and "I'm About to Become a Mother"—that contain the phrase "Who could ask for anything more?"

Snow White's sister is called Rose Red.

George W. Bush was the seventeenth U.S. state governor to become president.

Thirty-five percent of people who use personal ads for dating are already married.

In 1933, Mickey Mouse got 800,000 fan letters.

Sigmund Freud had a morbid fear of ferns.

A "penknife" was originally used to trim the tip of a quill.

In Alcatraz, Al Capone was inmate number 85.

California has issued driver's licenses to six people called Jesus Christ.

There are 22 stars in the Paramount logo.

Watermelon is a vegetable.

All the films nominated for Best Picture in 1999 were set more than fifty years before the films were released. The winner was *Shakespeare in Love;* the other nominees were *Saving Private Ryan, Life Is Beautiful, The Thin Red Line* and *Elizabeth.*

Kleenex tissues were originally used as filters in gas masks.

A twelve-ounce jar of peanut butter contains about 548 peanuts.

More people use blue toothbrushes than red ones.

People and Their Favorite Children's Book

Tony Blair: *Kidnapped*

Stephen Hawking: *She*

Gary Oldman: *Gulliver's Travels*

Harold Pinter: *Ulysses*

V. I. Lenin: *Uncle Tom's Cabin*

Ian Rankin: *Fox in Socks*

Ed McBain: *The Cat in the Hat*

Places That Have Been Called "the Venice of the North"

Hamburg, Germany

Stockholm, Sweden

Amsterdam, Holland

Manchester, England

Bruges, Belgium

Edinburgh, Scotland

Amiens, France

St. Petersburg, Russia

Birmingham, England

Giethoorn, Holland

Ottawa, Canada

Places That Have Been Called "the Venice of the South"

Fort Lauderdale, Florida

Mykonos, Greece

Zakynthos, Greece

Tarpon Springs, Florida

Sitangkai, Philippines

Sète, France

Places That Have Been Called "the Venice of the East"

Bangkok, Thailand

Alappuzha, India

Suzhou, China

Pii Mai, Laos

Udaipur, India

Lijiang, China

Shan, Myanmar

Places That Have Been Called "the Venice of the West"

Nantes, France

San Antonio, Texas

Galway, Ireland

Seattle, Washington

Onlys

Bill Clinton sent **only** two e-mails during his eight-year presidency. One was to John Glenn aboard the space shuttle and the other was to test the e-mail system.

Venus is the **only** planet that rotates clockwise.

The only dog ever to appear in a Shakespearean play was Crab in *The Two Gentlemen of Verona*.

The only Shakespeare play in which tennis balls appear is *Henry V*.

Canada is the only country not to win a gold medal in the summer Olympic Games while hosting the event.

Madrid and Valletta are the only European capital cities not on a river.

The only living tissue in the human body that contains no blood vessels is the transparent cornea of the eye.

Salt is the only rock humans can eat.

Diane Keaton was the only cast member of the original production of *Hair* not to take her clothes off onstage.

Honey is the only food that doesn't spoil.

The San Francisco cable cars are the only mobile national monuments in the United States.

Texas is the only U.S. state that permits residents to vote from space.

The only Nobel Prize winner to win an Oscar was George Bernard Shaw (for *Pygmalion*).

The bullfrog is the only animal that never sleeps.

In 1958, Zsa Zsa Gabor became the first—and **only**—recipient of a Golden Globe Award for Most Glamorous Actress (the award was never given again).

Hummingbirds are the only bird that can hover continuously.

Only six percent of the autographs in circulation from members of the Beatles are believed to be real.

Humans, ants and, to a lesser degree, chimpanzees are the **only** beings that wage organized warfare.

Herbert Hoover is the only U.S. president to have turned over his entire salary to charity.

The Only People to Have Won the Tony and the Oscar for the Same Role

José Ferrer for *Cyrano De Bergerac* (Tony: 1947/Oscar: 1950)

Shirley Booth for *Come Back, Little Sheba* (1950/1953)

Yul Brynner for *The King and I* (1952/1956)

Rex Harrison for *My Fair Lady* (1957/1964)

Anne Bancroft for *The Miracle Worker* (1960/1962)

Paul Scofield for *A Man for All Seasons* (1962/1966)

Jack Albertson for *The Subject Was Roses* (1965/1968)

Joel Grey for *Cabaret* (1967/1973)

Note: Lila Kedrova did it the other way around. She won a 1964 Oscar for *Zorba the Greek*, and twenty years later, won a Tony for the same role in *Zorba*.

Things Invented by Italians (and not all of them by Leonardo da Vinci)

The parachute, the camera obscura, the piano, the pretzel, the radio, the espresso machine, spectacles, the mariner compass, the thermometer, the barometer, magnets, the telescope, the condom, scissors, the mechanical calculator, the pedometer, the wind vane, Fibonacci numbers, natural plastic, the ice-cream cone

Everest Firsts

First ascent: May 29, 1953, by Edmund Hillary and Tenzing Norgay

First recorded deaths: seven Sherpas in an avalanche in 1922

First person to reach the summit a second time: Nawang Gombu Sherpa, on May 20, 1965

First woman to reach the summit: Junko Tabei, on May 16, 1975

First ascent without bottled oxygen: Peter Habeler and Reinhold Messner, on May 8, 1978

First winter ascent: Krzysztof Wielicki, on February 17, 1980

First blind person to reach the summit: Erik Weihenmayer, on May 25, 2001

Family

Céline Dion is one of fourteen children.

After divorcing Penelope Wilton, Daniel Massey married her sister Lindy.

Catherine Cookson's "sister" turned out to be her mother.

Pancho Gonzales was married to Andre Agassi's sister.

Kevin Spacey's older brother is a professional Rod Stewart impersonator.

Lenny Kravitz's mother played the part of Helen in *The Jeffersons*.

Naomi Watts is the daughter of Pink Floyd's former sound engineer (and her mobile phone has "Money" as its ring tone).

Cousins

Glenn Close and Brooke Shields

Brian Littrell and Kevin Richardson (both Backstreet Boys)

Alan Napier (Alfred in the *Batman* TV series) and Neville Chamberlain

Robert Aldrich and Nelson Rockefeller

Olympia Dukakis and Michael Dukakis

Brothers Joseph and Ralph Fiennes and Ranulph Fiennes

Tommy Lee Jones and Boxcar Willie

Mike Love and Brian Wilson

James Joyce and Adolphe Menjou

Michael Tilson Thomas and Paul Muni

Ramon Navarro and Dolores Del Rio

McLean Stevenson and Adlai Stevenson

Diane Ladd and Tennessee Williams

Marla Maples and Heather Locklear

Gloria Vanderbilt and Beatrice Straight

Madonna and Gwen Stefani (distant)

Oprah Winfrey and Elvis Presley (distant)

People with Famous Godparents

Zak Starkey (Ringo Starr's oldest son)—Keith Moon

Angelina Jolie—Maximilian Schell

Bryce Dallas Howard—Henry Winkler

Bijou Phillips—Andy Warhol

Phoebe Cates—Jacqueline Susann

Daniel Massey—Noël Coward

Sean Lennon—Elton John

Nicole Richie—Michael Jackson

Jake Gyllenhaal—Jaime Lee Curtis

People with Famous Ancestors

John Gielgud—Ellen Terry

Queen Sofia of Spain—Queen Victoria

Jason Patric—Jackie Gleason (grandfather)

Pat Boone—Daniel Boone

Nelson Eddy—Martin Van Buren

Sophie Dahl (Roald Dahl and Stanley Holloway—her grandfathers)

Christopher Plummer is the great-grandson of former Canadian prime minister John Abbott

John Kerry—King Henry III

Wayne Newton—Pocahontas

People and What Their Fathers Did for a Living

Sean Penn (film director—but was out of work after being blacklisted as a Communist)

Colin Farrell (stockbroker)

Anna Kournikova (wrestler)

Hugh Grant (carpet salesman)

Ben Affleck (social worker)

Damon Albarn (art-school lecturer)

Christian Bale (airline pilot)

Julia Ormond (software designer)

Sacha Baron Cohen (menswear-shop owner)

Jennifer Lopez (computer specialist at Guardian Life Insurance in New York City)

Leonardo DiCaprio (comic-book dealer)

Teri Hatcher (nuclear physicist)

Tom Cruise (electrical engineer)

John Cleese (Insurance salesman)

Andrew Lloyd Webber (organist)

Elizabeth Taylor (art dealer)

Neil Young (journalist)

Bob Geldof (traveling salesman)

Morrissey (hospital porter)

Mark Knopfler (architect)

Simon Le Bon (Foreign Office civil servant)

Will Smith (refrigeration engineer)

Oliver Stone (stockbroker)

Michael Jackson (crane driver)

Gloria Estefan (soldier in Cuban dictator Fulgencio Batista's bodyguard)

J. K. Rowling (engineer)

Jon Bon Jovi (hairdresser)

Brendan Fraser (tourism executive)

Leslie Nielsen (Royal Canadian Mountie)

Dan Brown (math professor)

People Whose Fathers Were Clergymen

Pearl Bailey, Ingmar Bergman, Erskine Caldwell, Alistair Cooke, George McGovern, Walter Mondale, Agnes Moorehead, Dean Rusk, Albert Schweitzer

People Whose Fathers Were Doctors

Lisa Kudrow, Reese Witherspoon, Sandra Bernhard, Fred Zinnemann, M. Night Shyamalan

People Whose Fathers Were Boxers

Rudy Giuliani, Jennifer Capriati, Frank Sinatra, Andre Agassi, Paul Weller

Brought up by a Single Parent

Barry Manilow, Billy Connolly, Fay Weldon, Keanu Reeves, Drew Barrymore, Mick Hucknall, Michael Crawford

People with Twin Brothers/Sisters

Scarlett Johansson (Hunter)

Gisele Bundchen (Patricia)

Plum Sykes (Lucy)

Ashton Kutcher (Michael)

Janel Moloney (Carey)

N.B.: Justin Timberlake had a twin named Laura, who died as a baby.

Girls Who Emancipated Themselves from Their Parents

Bijou Phillips—at 14

Alicia Silverstone—at 15 (When she was a child, her overactive imagination led her to claim that her parents were aliens and that her mother, an airline stewardess, was Olivia Newton-John.)

Michelle Williams—at 15

Juliette Lewis—at 14

Parents of Twins

Julia Roberts, Geena Davis (at age forty-seven), Madeleine Albright, Corbin Bernsen, Lou Diamond Phillips, Ed Asner, Henry Mancini, Rick Nelson, Meredith Baxter-Birney, Jim Brown, Andy Gibb (himself the brother of twins), Susan Hayward, Loretta Lynn, Otto Preminger, Nelson Rockefeller, Rip Torn, Holly Hunter (also at age forty-seven)

Grandparents of Twins

Tammy Wynette, George H. W. Bush

Famous People Who Were Born "Illegitimate"

T. E. Lawrence, William the Conqueror, Richard Wagner, Sophia Loren, Willy Brandt, Alec Guinness, Sarah Bernhardt, Leonardo da Vinci, Demi Moore, Macaulay Culkin, Ella Fitzgerald, Oprah Winfrey, Naomi Campbell, Coco Chanel, Fidel Castro, Franco Zeffirelli, the Duchess of Windsor, Tony O'Reilly, Marilyn Monroe, Eric Clapton, Billie Holiday, Mike Tyson, Saddam Hussein, Paul Cézanne, Jesse Jackson, Maria Montessori, August Strindberg, Juan Perón

People Who Never Knew Their Fathers

David Blaine, Charlene Tilton, Prince Michael of Kent, Natalia Makarova, Lee Trevino, Rod Steiger, Marilyn Monroe, Gerhard Schröder, Alec Guinness, Lee Harvey Oswald, Lord Byron

People with a German Parent

Eric Bana (mother)

Leonardo DiCaprio (mother)

Dennis Franz (father)

People with a French Parent

Joanne Harris (mother)

Mary Pierce (mother)

Jodie Foster (mother)

Claire Trevor
(father)

Things Said About France and the French

"When God created France, He realized that He had gone overboard in creating the most perfect place on Earth. So to balance it out, he created the French people." (Anonymous)

"Somewhere between the Angels and the French lies the rest of humanity" (Mark Twain)

"The French are just useless. They can't organize a piss-up in a brewery." (Elton John)

"We always have been, we are, and I hope that we always shall be detested in France." (The Duke of Wellington)

"France was a long despotism tempered by epigrams." (Thomas Carlyle)

"Going to war without France is like going deer

hunting without an accordion. You just leave a lot of useless, noisy baggage behind." (Jed Babbin)

"The reason French streets have trees planted down both sides is that the Germans like to march in the shade." (Anonymous)

"If you want to visit Paris, the best time to go is during August, when there aren't any French people there." (Kenneth Stilling)

People and the Subjects They Studied in College

J. K. Rowling—French and classics

Mira Sorvino—East Asian studies

Robin Williams—political science

Martin Short—social work

Thandie Newton—anthropology

Cate Blanchett—economics and fine arts

John Cleese—law

Glenn Close—anthropology

Hugh Grant—English

Brian May—physics

Lucy Liu—Asian languages and culture

Brooke Shields—French

Brad Pitt—journalism

Rowan Atkinson—electrical engineering

Paul Simon—English

Donald Fagen—English

Victoria Principal—law

Cindy Crawford—chemical engineering (on a full scholarship)

Lisa Kudrow—sociobiology (originally wanted to be a doctor like her father, a headache expert)

Numbers

Multiply 37,037 by any single number (1 to 9), then multiply that number by 3. Every digit in the answer will be the same as that first single number.

The number 17 is considered unlucky in Italy.

There are 318,979,564,000 possible combinations of the first four moves in chess.

One year contains 31,557,600 seconds.

"Eleven plus two" is a precise anagram of "twelve plus one."

Any number squared is equal to 4 (2 squared) more than the product of the numbers two digits to either side of it:

5 squared is 25 (3 x 7 is 21)

8 squared is 64 (6 x 10 is 60)

Any number squared is equal to 9 (3 squared) more than the product of the numbers three digits to either side of it: 5 squared is 25 (2 x 8 is 16)

8 squared is 64 (5 x 11 is 55) and so on

History

People didn't always say hello when they answered the phone. When the first regular phone service was established in 1878 in the United States, people said "Ahoy."

Of the 266 men who have been pope, 33 have died violently.

In eighteenth-century Britain, you could take out insurance against going to hell.

In 1915, William Wrigley Jr. sent chewing gum to everyone in the Chicago phone book.

Olive oil was once used for washing the body in Mediterranean countries.

Bagpipes were invented in Iran, then brought to Scotland by the Romans.

The world's youngest parents were eight and nine years old, and lived in China in 1910.

In England in the seventeenth century, married women had, on average, 13 children.

India was the richest country in the world until the time of British invasion in the early seventeenth century.

Benito Mussolini would ward off the evil eye by touching his testicles.

Stalin's left foot had webbed toes.

Between 1947 and 1959, 42 nuclear devices were detonated in the Marshall Islands in the Pacific Ocean.

Playing cards that were issued to British pilots in World War II could be soaked in water and unfolded to reveal a map in the event of capture.

In Egypt in the late nineteenth century, mummies were used as fuel for locomotives, since wood and coal were scarce but mummies were plentiful.

Louis IV of France had a stomach the size of two normal stomachs.

Paul Gauguin was a laborer on the Panama Canal.

It cost $7 million to build the *Titanic* and $200 million to make a film about it.

Two dogs (a Pomerian—name unknown—and a Pekingese called Sun Yat-sen) survived the sinking of the *Titanic*.

King Louis XIX ruled France for fifteen minutes.

Japan did not send an ambassador to another nation until 1860.

In sixteenth-century Turkey, drinking coffee was punishable by death.

Leprosy is the world's oldest known disease, dating back to 1350 B.C.

Stone wheels several feet in diameter were once used as currency by the Yap Islanders of Micronesia.

In the Middle Ages, the highest court in France ordered the execution of a cow for injuring someone.

The passion fruit was named by Spanish missionaries to whom the plant suggested the nails and thorns of Christ's suffering (or Passion) at the crucifixion.

Charles Dickens earned as much for his lectures as he did for all his twenty novels combined.

In medieval Japan it was fashionable for women to have black teeth.

When the *Mayflower* was no longer needed as a ship, it was taken apart and rebuilt as a barn.

Russia's Peter the Great taxed men who wore a beard.

In the nineteenth century, in an attempt to debunk the myth that Friday was an unlucky day for mariners, the British navy named a new ship *HMS Friday*, found a Captain Friday to command it and sent it to sea on a Friday. Neither ship nor crew was heard of again.

Apollo 11 had thirty seconds of fuel left when it landed.

In eighteenth-century English gambling dens, there was an employee whose only job it was to swallow the dice in the event of a police raid.

The formal name for the Pony Express was the Central Overland California & Pike's Peak Express Company.

In 1930, Grace Robin, a model, demonstrated contact lenses for the first time.

The streets of ancient Mesopotamia were literally knee-deep in rubbish, since there was no effective way of getting rid of it.

In ancient Rome a crooked nose was considered to indicate leadership potential.

George Washington's false teeth were carved from hippopotamus ivory and cows' teeth and fixed together with metal springs.

Noblewomen in ancient Egypt were given a few days to ripen after death in order not to provide temptation for the embalmers to violate the corpse.

The gold earrings many sailors wore were intended to pay for a decent burial upon their death.

St. Patrick, the patron saint of Ireland, was not Irish.

The world's oldest active parliamentary body is the Icelandic Althing, which first met before the year 1000.

The Chinese used fingerprints as a method of identification as far back as A.D. 700.

In 1386, a pig was hanged in public in France for "murdering" a child.

The Puritans brought three times as much beer as water with them on their journey to the New World.

In the thirteenth century, the Pope set quality standards for pasta.

In ancient Japan a man could divorce his wife if he discovered that she was left-handed.

Queen Elizabeth I was responsible for heels being added to shoes: she wanted the royal family to have additional stature.

The ancient Egyptians used to bury mummified mice with their mummified cats.

Andrew Jackson's pet parrot swore at the president's funeral and was duly removed.

When Thomas Edison died in 1941, Henry Ford captured his last dying breath in a bottle.

All the UN Secretaries-General Since Its Formation

Trygve Lie (Norway) 1946–53

Dag Hammarskjöld (Sweden) 1953–61

U Thant (Burma) 1962–71

Kurt Waldheim (Austria) 1972–81

Javier Pérez de Cuéllar (Peru) 1982–91

Boutros Boutros-Ghali (Egypt) 1992–96

Kofi Annan (Ghana) 1997–

Birds, Etc.

Pigeons can fly 600 miles in a day.

Flamingos get their color from their food, tiny green algae that turn pink during digestion.

There are giant bats in Indonesia with a wingspan of nearly 6 feet.

The common little brown bat of North America is, for its size, the world's longest-lived mammal. It can live to the age of 32.

Baby robins eat 14 feet of earthworms per day.

A duck has three eyelids.

Chickens, ducks and ostriches are eaten before they're born and after they're dead.

A robin's egg is blue, but if you put it in vinegar, it turns yellow after a month.

Penguins have sex twice a year.

Big Ben lost five minutes one day when a flock of starlings perched on the minute hand.

To keep cool, ostriches urinate on their legs.

Crows have the biggest brains of any bird, relative to body size.

Birds need gravity in order to swallow.

A parrot's beak can exert a force of 350 pounds per square inch as it snaps shut.

Many species of bird mate on the wing. They fly high and then mate on the descent.

Chickens that lay brown eggs have red earlobes.

White cockatoos can be sexed by eye color. The males have black irises and an invisible pupil; the females have a paler iris with a visible pupil.

The ostrich yolk is the largest single cell in the world.

The pallid bat has immunity to the poison of the scorpions upon which it feeds.

Some birds have eyes that weigh more than their brains.

Frog-eating bats find and identify edible frogs by listening for their mating calls. Frogs counter this by hiding and using short calls that are hard to locate.

Fishing bats use echolocation so well they can detect a hair's breadth of minnow fin above a pond surface.

Vampire bats adopt orphans and have been known to risk their lives to share food with less fortunate roostmates.

Andean condors can live for 70 years.

Penguins have an organ above their eyes that converts seawater to freshwater.

Farmed turkeys can't fly, but wild turkeys can (for short distances).

The male house wren builds several nests, from which his mate selects one.

In Africa, ostriches are used to herd sheep.

An ostrich egg is equal in size to 24 chicken eggs.

Flamingos can live for fifty years.

Migrating geese fly in a V formation to conserve energy, with each goose taking its turn to lead the group.

The hummingbird, the kingfisher and the grebe are all birds that can't walk.

Bird Names

Jackass penguin, wandering albatross, red-faced shag, blue-footed booby, intermediate egret, short-toed lark, oven-bird, solitary sandpiper, least bittern, adjutant stork, sacred ibis, horned screamer, smew, killdeer, turnstone, beach thick-knee, laughing gull, fairy tern, masked love-bird, roadrunner, screech owl, large frogmouth, chimney swift, train-bearing hermit, turquoise-browed motmot, toco toucan, barred woodcreeper, spotted antbird, cock-of-the-rock, ornate umbrellabird, vermilion flycatcher, reddish plantcutter, superb lyrebird, racquet-tailed drongo, crestless gardener, satin bowerbird, magnificent riflebird, spotted creeper, striped jungle babbler, fairy bluebird, noisy friarbird, bananaquit, painted bunting, social weaver, red-legged honeycreeper, junglefowl, northern shoveler, wrinkled hornbill, blue-bearded bee-eater, dollarbird, edible-nest swiftlet, buffy fish owl, little stint, changeable hawk eagle, straw-headed bulbul, spectacled spiderhunter

Patrons

Stephen Fry—Norwich Playhouse

Richard Attenborough—Kingsley Hall Community Centre

Catherine Zeta-Jones—Wales's Longfields Association

Roger Daltrey—Teenage Cancer Trust

People and Their Classmates' Ratings

James Gandolfini—voted Best Looking

Billy Crystal—voted Best Personality

Lorraine Bracco—voted Ugliest Girl

   Sally Field—voted Class Clown

Heather Graham—voted Most Talented

Valedictorians

Cindy Crawford

Alicia Keys

Jodie Foster

Paul Robeson

Genuine Answers Given by High School Students on Science Tests

The body consists of three parts: the brainium, the borax and the abominable cavity. The brainium contains the brain, the borax contains the heart and lungs, and the abominable cavity contains the bowels, of which there are five—*a, e, i, o* and *u.*

   The pistol of a flower is its only protection against insects.

When you breathe, you inspire. When you do not breathe, you expire.

When you smell an odorless gas, it is probably carbon monoxide.

Dew is formed on leaves when the sun shines down on them and makes them perspire.

Nitrogen is not found in Ireland because it is not found in a free state.

H_2O is hot water, and CO_2 is cold water.

To collect fumes of sulfur, hold a deacon over a flame in a test tube.

Blood flows down one leg and up the other.

Water is composed of two gins, Oxygin and Hydrogin. Oxygin is pure gin. Hydrogin is gin and water.

A fossil is an extinct animal. The older it is, the more extinct it is.

The Moon is a planet just like the Earth, only it is even deader.

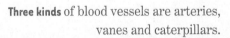

Mushrooms always grow in damp places, and so they look like umbrellas.

Three kinds of blood vessels are arteries, vanes and caterpillars.

Respiration is composed of two acts, first inspiration, then expectoration.

Artificial insemination is when the farmer does it to the cow instead of the bull.

A supersaturated solution is one that holds more than it can hold.

The **skeleton** is what is left after the insides have been taken out and the outsides have been taken off. The purpose of the skeleton is something to hitch meat to.

Before giving a blood transfusion, find out if the blood is affirmative or negative.

A **permanent set of teeth** consists of eight canines, eight cuspids, two molars and eight cuspidors.

The tides are a fight between the Earth and Moon. All water tends toward the moon, because there is no water in the Moon, and nature abhors a vacuum. I forget where the sun joins in this fight.

Many women believe that an alcoholic binge will have no ill effects on the unborn fetus, but that is a large misconception.

Germinate: to become a naturalized German.

Momentum: what you give a person when they are going away.

To remove dust from the eye, pull the eye down over the nose.

To prevent contraception, wear a condominium.

To keep milk from turning sour, keep it in the cow.

People Who Were Expelled from School

Jeff Stryker (for "standing up for a retard")

Chevy Chase (from Haverford College, for taking a cow onto the third floor of a campus building)

Adam Clayton (from a boarding school)

Alain Delon (from many schools)

Redd Foxx (on the first day, for throwing a book at the teacher)

Brandon Lee (for misbehaving)

Shane MacGowan (from Westminster, for using drugs)

Rudolph Valentino (from many schools)

Harvey Keitel (for repeated truancy)

Johnny Rotten (from a Catholic comprehensive near Pentonville prison)

Things Said About School

"Show me a man who has enjoyed his schooldays and I'll show you a bully and a bore." (Robert Morley)

"The philosophy of the schoolroom in one generation will be the philosophy of government in the next." (Abraham Lincoln)

"You don't appreciate a lot of stuff in school until you get older. Little things like being spanked every day by a middle-aged woman: stuff you pay good money for in later life." (Emo Phillips)

"He who opens a school door closes a prison." (Victor Hugo)

"Don't let schooling interfere with your education." (Mark Twain)

"I hated school. Even to this day, when I see a school bus, it's just depressing to me. The poor little kids." (Dolly Parton)

"The schools ain't what they used to be and never was." (Will Rogers)

"If there were no schools to take the children away from home part of the time, the insane asylums would be filled with mothers." (Edward Howe)

"Education is what remains after one has forgotten what one has learned in school." (Albert Einstein)

"A child educated only at school is an uneducated child." (George Santayana)

"To sentence a man of true genius to the drudgery of a school is to put a racehorse on a treadmill." (Samuel Taylor Coleridge)

"Everyone is in awe of the lion tamer in a cage with half a dozen lions—everyone but a school bus driver." (Laurence Peter)

"I won't say ours was a tough school, but we had our own coroner. We used to write essays like: What I'm going to be if I grow up." (Lenny Bruce)

Genuine Notes Sent by Parents to School to Explain Their Children's Absence

Please excuse Joey on Friday; he had loose vowels.

My daughter wouldn't come to school on Monday because she was tired. She spent the weekend with some marines.

Dear school: Please exkuse John for being absent on January 28, 29, 30, 31, 32 and 33.

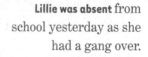

Lillie was absent from school yesterday as she had a gang over.

Please excuse Johnnie for being. It was his father's fault.

I kept Billie home to do Christmas shopping because I didn't know what size she wears.

Please excuse Sara for being absent. She was sick, and I had her shot.

People Who Were Fat as Children

Kate Winslet (her childhood nickname was Blubber)

Meatloaf (weighed more when he was ten than he does now)

John Malkovich (lost weight by eating only Jell-O)

Sandy Lyle (his nickname was "Podge")

Orlando Bloom (after breaking his leg skiing: "I sat at home really depressed and ate biscuits and chocolate")

Silent film star Roscoe "Fatty" Arbuckle (weighed sixteen pounds at birth)

People Who Appeared in Commercials as Children

Reese Witherspoon (appeared in a TV commercial when she was seven for a local Nashville florist)

Lindsay Lohan (Pizza Hut, the Gap, Wendy's, Jell-O)

Pejorative Fruits

Fruit—old-time slang for a homosexual

Gooseberry—a third party on a date

Plum—a person prone to mistakes

Prune—an elderly person

Turnip—an idiot

Lemon—a chronically defective object

Nut—a psychopath

Grapes—hemorrhoids

Limey—U.S. slang for the English

Fig—an inconsequential person

Achievements After the Age of 80

At the age of 80, George Burns won an Oscar for his role in *The Sunshine Boys*. He died at the age of 100, having retired from live performing only three years before.

At the age of 82, Winston Churchill published part one of his four-part *History of the English-Speaking Peoples*.

At the age of 84, William Gladstone was prime minister of Britain.

At the age of 84, W. Somerset Maugham published a collection of essays entitled *Points of View*.

At the age of 85, Mae West starred in the film *Sextet*.

At the age of 87, Francis Rous was awarded the 1966 Nobel Prize for Medicine.

At the age of 87, John Gielgud starred in the film *Prospero's Books*.

At the age of 88, Michelangelo was still sculpting.

At the age of 91, Eamon de Valera was president of Ireland.

At the age of 95, the American pianist Arthur Rubinstein gave a public concert.

At the age of 95, John Mills appeared in the film *Bright Young Things*.

People Who Published Their Diaries

Evelyn Waugh, Antony Sher, Roger Moore, Andy Warhol, Vaslav Nijinsky, Jeffrey Archer, Brian Eno, Che Guevara, Samuel Pepys, Alec Guinness, Anaïs Nin

Animals, Etc.

Sheep will not drink running water.

Cows can smell odors 6 miles away.

Every lion's muzzle is unique—no two lions have the same pattern of whiskers.

Every Holstein's spots are unique—no two cows have the same pattern of spots.

Deer can't eat hay.

The horny pad on the underside of a horse's hoof is called a frog. The frog peels off several times a year with new growth.

Cats can hear ultrasound.

The New Mexican whiptail lizard reproduces asexually, laying eggs that are clones of the mother. A courtship ritual is required between two female lizards in order to encourage the release of the eggs.

Giant pandas can eat 83 pounds of bamboo a day.

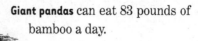

Male monkeys go bald in much the same way that men do.

You can tell a turtle's gender by the noise it makes: males grunt, females hiss.

Reindeer like bananas.

The ferret was domesticated five hundred years before the cat. The female ferret is called a jill.

A camel's backbone is as straight as a horse's.

The tuatara lizard of New Zealand has 3 eyes—two that are positioned normally and an extra on top of its head.

The woolly mammoth had tusks almost 16 feet long.

The sitatunga antelope is amphibious. Its water-adapted hooves are awkward on dry land.

A laboratory mouse put on a treadmill for a night runs for five miles.

The world's smallest dog—the Teacup Chihuahua – weighs less than a pound when fully grown.

A bear has 42 teeth.

The black bear has a blue tongue.

Hamsters like crickets as food.

Montana mountain goats can butt heads so hard that their hooves fall off.

Polar bears cover their black noses with their paws for better camouflage.

A pig sleeps on its right side.

There are only three types of snakes on the island of Tasmania, and all three are deadly poisonous.

A blind chameleon still changes color to match its environment.

Alligators cannot move backward.

Four hundred quarter-pound hamburgers can be made out of one cow.

Armadillos have four babies at a time, and they are always all of the same sex.

A zebra is white with black stripes.

The longest snake is the royal python, which can grow to 35 feet long.

When opossums are playing possum, they are not "playing"—they pass out from sheer terror.

If you are chased by a crocodile, run in a serpentine fashion—a crocodile isn't good at making sharp turns.

Crocodiles never outgrow the pool in which they live. If you put a baby croc in an aquarium, it would be small for the rest of its life.

Squirrels can climb faster than they can run.

The kinkajou, which belongs to the same family as the raccoon, has a prehensile tail that is twice the length of its body. At night it wraps itself up in its tail to sleep.

An adult hippo can bite a 12-foot adult male crocodile in half and can open its mouth wide enough to fit a 4-foot human child inside. A hippo can also outrun a man.

The world's smallest mammal (where skull size is the defining factor) is the bumblebee bat of Thailand.

Rabbits and parrots can both see behind themselves without turning their head.

A monkey was once tried and convicted in Indiana for smoking a cigarette.

Camels chew in a figure- eight pattern.

A kangaroo can jump only when its tail is touching the ground.

At full speed a cheetah takes 26-foot strides.

The honey badger in Africa can withstand bee stings that would kill another animal.

Eighty percent of the noise a hippo makes is made underwater.

A cat uses its whiskers to determine if a space is big enough to squeeze through.

Koalas rarely drink water but get fluids from the eucalyptus leaves they eat. In fact, *"koala"* is believed to mean "no drink" in an Aboriginal language. Koalas have no natural predators.

A dairy cow gives nearly 200,000 glasses of milk in her lifetime.

You can tell if a pig's sick: it stops curling its tail.

Camels will refuse to carry loads that aren't properly balanced.

Chinchilla hairs are so fine that it would take 500 to equal the thickness of a single human hair.

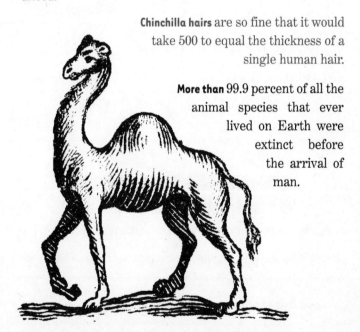

More than 99.9 percent of all the animal species that ever lived on Earth were extinct before the arrival of man.

There are fewer than 1,000 Bactrian camels left in the wild.

You can smell the odor of a skunk a mile away.

Koalas sleep 18 to 20 hours a day.

A horse eats about 7 times its own weight a year.

Sheep can recognize faces.

Cats have the largest eyes of all mammals (proportional to their size).

It takes about 50 hours for a snake to digest a frog.

Beavers mate for life.

The typical elephant produces 50 pounds of dung a day.

Until he's about 21 years old, the male Indian elephant isn't interested in female elephants.

Elephants sometimes remain standing after they die.

Animal Hybrids

Mule: cross between a male donkey and a female horse

Hinny: cross between a male horse and a female donkey

Zeedonk: cross between a zebra and a donkey

Wolfdog: cross between a wolf and a dog

Liger: cross between a male lion and a female tiger

Tigon: cross between a male tiger and a female lion

Cama: cross between a camel and a llama

Wolphin: cross between a whale and a dolphin (only one in existence)

People and Their Pets

PERSON	PET	NAME
Reese Witherspoon	Dog: bulldog	Frank Sinatra
Pamela Anderson	Dog: golden retriever	Star
Liv Tyler	Dog: King Charles Spaniel	Neal
Hilary Duff	Dog: fox terrier/ Chihuahua	Little Dog
Mariah Carey	Dogs: shih tzus	Bing and Bong
	Jack Russell	Jack
	Yorkshire terrier	Ginger

PERSON	PET	NAME
Adrien Brody	Dog: Chihuahua	Ceelo
Vanilla Ice	Wallaroo: a kangaroo-wallaby cross	Bucky
	Goat	Pancho
Michael Stipe	Dog: black-and-white terrier	Helix
Natascha McElhone	Cat	Soup
Kate Bosworth	Cats	Louise and Dusty
Jake Gyllenhaal	Dog	300 Radley

A Guide to Rabbits

Rabbits are sociable creatures often found living in large groups in underground burrows or warrens. A colony of 407 rabbits was once found, with a warren that had 2,080 exits.

Most rabbits are cottontails.

A rabbit's eyes are capable of seeing in every direction, making it possible to watch predators in the air and on the ground.

Rabbits are more closely related to horses than they are to rodents or mice.

Rabbits twitch their noses constantly because they depend on their sense of smell to warn them of danger.

The Ryukyu rabbit and Mexico's volcano rabbit are among the rarest mammals in the world.

The highest a rabbit has ever jumped is 39.2 inches.

The only film Joan Rivers ever directed was entitled *Rabbit Test* (1978).

A farmer introduced 24 wild rabbits into Australia in 1859. There are now an estimated 300 million rabbits there.

Famous rabbits include: Brer Rabbit; The White Rabbit (in *Alice's Adventures in Wonderland*); Hazel; Fiver; Bigwig and friends. (in *Watership Down*); Peter Rabbit; Benjamin Bunny; Bucky O'Hare; Rabbit (in A. A. Milne's Winnie-the-Pooh stories); Peter Cottontail; Bugs Bunny; Harvey (James Stewart's imaginary best friend in the 1950 film *Harvey*); Lola (in the film *Space Jam*); the Monster of Caer Bannog (in the film *Monty Python and the Holy Grail*); Oswald the Lucky Rabbit; Roger Rabbit; Thumper (in the film *Bambi*); Babs Bunny (in Steven Spielberg's *Tiny Toon Adventures*); Bean Bunny (in *The Muppets*); Benny Rabbit (in *Sesame* Street); Frank (in the cult film *Donnie Darko*); the Easter Bunny

Before Fame

Paul Bettany used to perform for donations on Westminster Bridge.

Lemmy, the lead singer of Motörhead, used to be a roadie for Jimi Hendrix.

Tracey Ullman used to be a member of the Second Generation dance group.

Elton John once auditioned for the group King Crimson.

Joseph Fiennes used to be a theater usher and once told off Helen Mirren for not sitting down, without realizing that she was one of the actresses.

Nathan Lane used to work delivering singing telegrams.

Stephen Sondheim once tried out as a contestant on *The $64,000 Question* (answering questions on John Ford films).

Errol Flynn used to work on a farm where he had to castrate sheep by biting off their testicles.

Minnie Driver attended finishing schools in Paris and Grenoble.

At one point Jim Carrey and his family lived out of their car/trailer.

Michael Crawford took his stage name off a biscuit tin.

Stockard Channing received a substantial inheritance at the age of fifteen after the death of her shipping-magnate father.

Hugh Grant appeared as a contestant in the British TV quiz show *Top of the Form*.

Colin Farrell auditioned for the Irish boy band Boyzone but didn't get in.

As a young woman, Lorraine Bracco was once asked to pose nude for Salvador Dalí, but she refused.

Danny Kaye was sacked from his job at an insurance company after accidentally paying a claimant $40,000 instead of $4,000.

Nicole Kidman and Naomi Watts both attended North Sydney Girls' High School.

Jack Osbourne, Robert Carlyle and Catherine Zeta-Jones left school without any qualifications.

Keanu Reeves managed a pasta shop in Toronto, Canada.

People and What They Did Before Becoming Famous

Angelina Jolie—Embalmer

Afroman—Worked in a chicken factory

Jason Biggs—Subway sandwich maker

Ricky Gervais—Pizza delivery boy

Shane MacGowan—Worked in a record shop

Christie Brinkley—Painter

Gabriel Byrne—Plumber's assistant, apprentice chef, archaeologist, teacher

Paul Newman—Encyclopedia salesman

Jon Bon Jovi—Worked in Burger King

Giorgio Armani—Window dresser

Danny DeVito—Janitor

Keanu Reeves—Managed a pasta shop

Former Librarians

Mao Tse-tung, Casanova, Philip Larkin, August Strindberg, David Hockney, J. Edgar Hoover, Pope Pius XI, Laura Bush, Howard W. Koch, Boris Pasternak

Former Playboy Bunnies

Debbie Harry, Lauren Hutton, Gloria Steinem (on an undercover assignment)

Trained as Engineers

Rowan Atkinson, Walter Huston, Ringo Starr, Yasser Arafat

Trained as Dancers

Madonna, Jennifer Lopez, Keira Knightley, Ken Russell, Victoria Principal, Brigitte Bardot, Suzanne Vega

Former Journalists

Frederick Forsyth, Chrissie Hynde, Evelyn Waugh, Ali MacGraw, Jilly Cooper, Mark Knopfler, Patrick Stewart

People Who Lived on a Kibbutz

Isla Fisher, Annie Leibovitz, Bob Hoskins, Ruby Wax, Mike Leigh, Lynne Reid Banks (for nine years), Uri Geller, Dr. Ruth Westheimer, Simon Le Bon, Sandra Bernhard, Jerry Seinfeld

Former Roommates

David Lynch and Peter Wolf

Nastassja Kinski and Demi Moore

Taki Theodoracopoulos and Peter Lawford

Johnny Rotten and Sid Vicious

People Who Used to Work in Shops

Mick Fleetwood (Liberty)

Glenda Jackson (Boots)

George Michael (BHS)

People Who Used to be Waiters/Waitresses

Annie Lennox, Rickie Lee Jones, Jacqueline Bisset, Diana Rigg, Ellen Barkin, Paula Abdul, Alec Baldwin, Antonio Banderas, Jennifer Aniston, Ellen DeGeneres, Angela Bassett (a singing waitress), Mariah Carey, Dustin Hoffman, Julianna Margulies, Edward Norton, Barbra Streisand, Russell Crowe, Kristin Davis, Julianne Moore, Robin Wright Penn, Emily Watson, Allison Janney, Julia Ormond, Renée Zellweger (in a topless bar—although she refused to take off her bra)

People Who Qualified as Lawyers

Margaret Thatcher, Mohandas Gandhi, Hoagy Carmichael, Tony Blair, Fidel Castro, Rossano Brazzi, Jerry Springer, Erle Stanley Gardner, Otto Preminger, Geraldo Rivera

N.B.: Bing Crosby, Estelle Parsons and Cole Porter all studied law without getting their degrees.

People Who've Worked in Advertising

Ridley Scott (as a director—e.g., on Hovis)

Fay Weldon (as a copywriter)

Salman Rushdie (as a copywriter)

Alec Guinness (as a copywriter working on campaigns for Rose's Lime Juice, razors and radio valves)

Len Deighton (as a copywriter)

Spike Lee (as a copywriter)

Martin Amis (as a copywriter)

Charlie Watts (as a designer)

Tim Allen (as a creative director)

Sela Ward (as an art director)

Hugh Grant (as an advertising account executive)

Things Said About Advertising

"Advertising is legalized lying." (H. G. Wells)

"Half the money I spend on advertising is wasted, and the trouble is, I don't know which half." (Lord Leverhulme)

"Advertising agency: eighty-five percent confusion and fifteen percent commission." (Fred Allen)

"Time spent in the advertising business seems to create a permanent deformity, like the Chinese habit of foot-binding." (Dean Acheson)

"Advertising is a racket. Its constructive contribution to humanity is exactly zero." (F. Scott Fitzgerald)

"Advertising is the art of making whole lies out of half truths." (Edgar A. Shoaff)

"Advertising is the rattling of a stick inside a swill bucket." (George Orwell)

"Advertising may be described as the science of arresting the human intelligence long enough to get money from it." (Stephen Leacock)

People and the Products They Advertised in Japan

Sting (Kirin beer)

Sean Connery (Itoh sausages)

Brad Pitt (Toyota—paid $1 million per day for three days' work)

Jay Kay (Sony Walkman)

Keanu Reeves (Suntory whiskey)

Ewan McGregor (Bobson jeans)

Arnold Schwarzenegger (Nissin Cup Noodles and DirecTV)

Brooke Shields (Aloe Mine)

Winona Ryder (Subaru Impreza)

Ringo Starr (Ringosutta applesauce)

Dennis Hopper (Tsumura Bathclin, a bath salt)

Harrison Ford (Kirin beer)

Sylvester Stallone (Itoh sausages)

Charlie Sheen (Tokyo Gas)

Madonna (Jun liquor)

Gene Hackman (Kirin beer)

Richard Gere (Japan Airlines)

Bruce Willis (NTT mobile phones)

Michael Bolton (Georgia coffee)

Jodie Foster (Honda Civic)

David Bowie (Takara Shochu)

Kevin Costner (Kirin beer)

Boy George (Takara Shochu)

Jeffrey Archer (Suntory)

Natalie Imbruglia (got her big break at age sixteen as the Pineapple Princess in a Japanese chewing gum commercial)

Bizarre Place-Names

Agenda (Wisconsin)

Asbestos (Canada)

Banana (Australia)

Belcher (Louisiana)

Bird-in-Hand (Pennsylvania)

Blubberhouses (United Kingdom)

Boom (Belgium)

Boring (Oregon)

Chicken (Alaska)

Chunky (Mississippi)

Ding Dong (Texas)

71

Drain (Oregon)

Eye (United Kingdom)

Hell (Norway)

How (Wisconsin)

Howlong (Australia)

Humpty Doo (Australia)

Lower Slaughter (United Kingdom)

Loyal (Oklahoma)

Luck (Wisconsin)

Mars (Pennsylvania)

Matching Tye (United Kingdom)

Medicine Hat (Canada)

Moron (Mongolia)

Nasty (United Kingdom)

Natters (Austria)

Normal (Illinois)

Parachute (Colorado)

Peculiar (Missouri)

Pity Me (United Kingdom)

Pussy (France)

Puzzletown (Pennsylvania)

Rottenegg (Austria)

Rough and Ready (California)

Secretary (Maryland)

Silly (Belgium)

Simmering (Austria)

Siren (Wisconsin)

Smackover (Arkansas)

Snapfinger (Georgia)

Spit Junction (Australia)

Surprise (Arizona)

Tiddleywink (Wiltshire)

Tightwad (Missouri)

Toast (North Carolina)

Truth or Consequences (New Mexico)

Useless Loop (Australia)

Vulcan (Canada)

Wham (United Kingdom)

Zig Zag (Australia)

Things Said About Australia and the Australians

"Australia has more things that will kill you than anywhere else." (Bill Bryson)

"You don't say 'cheers' when you drink a cup of tea in the bush, you say, 'Christ, the flies!'" (Prince Charles)

"Australia is a huge rest home where no unwelcome news is wafted onto the pages of the worst newspapers in the world." (Germaine Greer)

"Australians can, and do, quite readily and often in my experience, throw off all their 180 years of civilized nationhood." (Ted Dexter)

"[Australians are] violently loud alcoholic roughnecks whose idea of fun is to throw up in your car." (P. J. O'Rourke)

"Australia may be the only country in the world in which the word 'academic' is regularly used as a term of abuse." (Leonie Kramer)

"A broad school of Australian writing has based itself on the assumption that Australia not only has a history worth bothering about but that all the history worth bothering about happened in Australia." (Clive James)

"It's so empty and featureless—like a newspaper that has been entirely censored." (Robert Morley)

"The Australian temper is at bottom grim: it is as though the hot sun has dried up his nature." (Sir Neville Cardus)

"To live in Australia permanently is rather like going to a party and dancing all night with one's mother." (Barry Humphries)

"When I look at the map and see what an ugly country Australia is, I feel that I want to go there and see if it cannot be changed into a more beautiful form." (Oscar Wilde)

Things That Come from Australia

Mimosa, emus, macadamia nuts, koala bears, kangaroos, didgeridoos, Aussie Rules football, acacia, bandicoots, wombats, Castlemaine XXXX, Foster's, dingoes

People

Charisma Carpenter is an avid skydiver.

Sean Connery appeared in a political broadcast for the Scottish Nationalist Party.

Dick Van Dyke is ambidextrous.

William H. Macy believes that he was a golden retriever in a previous life.

Walt Disney's autograph bears no resemblance to the one in the famous Disney logo.

Kirstie Alley bans anyone wearing perfume in her house (because of its destructive effect on the ozone layer).

Woody Allen eats out every day of the year.

Frank Sinatra was voted "Worst Autograph Giver" by *Autograph Collector* magazine.

Jack Palance has never watched any of his own films.

Paul Newman stopped signing autographs "when I was standing at a urinal at Sardi's and a guy came up with a pen and paper. I wondered: do I wash first and then shake hands?"

Before marrying his wife, Jay Leno lived (at different times) with five women who were all born on September 5.

Noah Wyle is a Civil War buff.

Wynonna took her name from the town of Winona, Arizona, mentioned in the song "Route 66."

Backstreet Boy A. J. McLean has never blown his nose ("When it comes to anything mucus-oriented or phlegm or someone spitting, I gag").

Harpo Marx once tried to adopt child star Shirley Temple.

Eddie Murphy crosses himself before he enters elevators.

Matt Groening incorporated his initials into the drawing of Homer Simpson: there's an *M* in his hair and his ear is the letter *G*.

Ben Affleck's reformed-alcoholic father, Tim, became Robert Downey Jr.'s drug counselor.

Jennifer Lopez takes along her own sheets when she stays at a hotel.

Lucy Liu practices the martial art of kali-eskrima-silat (knife and stick fighting).

Robert Duvall has a passion for the tango and practices every day.

Dooley Wilson, who appeared as Sam the piano player in *Casablanca*, was in fact a drummer and not a pianist.

Maurice Chevalier had a clause in his contract with Paramount Pictures that if he ever lost his French accent, they could terminate the contract.

Sheryl Crow's front two teeth are fake—her own were knocked out when she tripped on stage.

Thomas Jefferson introduced ice cream to the United States.

Vincent van Gogh cut off his left ear. His "Self-Portrait with Bandaged Ear" shows the right one bandaged because he painted the mirror image.

Arnold Schoenberg suffered from triskaidekaphobia, the fear of the number thirteen. He died thirteen minutes from midnight on Friday the 13th.

Isaac Newton was just twenty-three years old when he discovered the law of universal gravitation.

Harrison Ford, Angelina Jolie, Patrick Swayze and Gene Hackman have all qualified as pilots.

Greg Norman, Lorraine Bracco and Olivia Newton-John all own vineyards.

After Ludwig van Beethoven went deaf, he could still hear his music by resting one end of a stick on the piano and holding the other end in his teeth.

Janis Joplin sucked her thumb until the age of eight.

Al Green's father fed him his pet goat Billy for dinner.

Albert Einstein couldn't speak properly until he was nine (his parents thought he might be retarded).

Neil Diamond went around Australia wearing a shirt that said I'M NOT NEIL DIAMOND—I JUST LOOK LIKE HIM.

Spencer Tracy's 1937 Best Actor Oscar (for *Captains Courageous*) was mistakenly engraved To DICK TRACY.

Celebrities Who Bought Other Celebrities' Houses

Elizabeth Taylor lives in a house once owned by Frank Sinatra.

Gangsta rapper 50 Cent bought Mike Tyson's seventeen-acre estate in Farmington, Connecticut.

Brittany Murphy bought Britney Spears's Hollywood Hills house.

Doris Duke bought Rudolph Valentino's house.

David Blaine lives in a Gothic-style manor house in the Hollywood Hills that used to belong to Harry Houdini.

Madonna and Guy Ritchie own Ashcombe House, Wiltshire—where Cecil Beaton lived from 1930 to 1945.

Gwyneth Paltrow and Chris Martin bought Kate Winslet's North London home in Belsize Park.

Mackenzie Crook of *The Office* bought Peter Sellers's old house in Muswell Hill.

Eddie Murphy bought the house on Benedict Canyon Drive that was once owned by Cher.

Paul McCartney bought Courtney Love's old house in Los Angeles.

Vegans

Fiona Apple, Kate Moss, Lindsay Wagner, Daryl Hannah, Casey Affleck, Linda Blair, Julia Stiles, Tobey Maguire, Noah Wyle

People and their tattoos

Kelis: giant orchid on her backside

Ewan McGregor: heart-and-dagger on his right shoulder

Elijah Wood: Elvish symbol on his hip

George Shultz: tiger on his bottom

Princess Stephanie of Monaco: dragon on her hip

Pamela Anderson: Tommy Lee's name on her wedding finger

Johnny Depp: Winona Forever on his arm (changed to Wino Forever when he and Winona Ryder split up)

Joan Baez: flower on her back

Kelly McGillis: red rose on her ankle

Brigitte Nielsen: heart on her bottom

Christy Turlington: heart on her ankle

Whoopi Goldberg: the *Peanuts'* Woodstock on her breast

Alyssa Milano: SRW, the initials of her ex-fiancé, on her right ankle

Natasha Henstridge: intertwined male and female symbols on her coccyx; bearded lion with crown—her astrological sign is Leo—on her bottom

Rose McGowan: woman on her right shoulder

People Who Live/Lived on Houseboats

Frederick Forsyth, Richard Branson, Pink Floyd's David Gilmour

People Who've Made Mr. Blackwell's Annual "Worst-Dressed" List

Anne Robinson (2001): "Harry Potter in Drag . . . a Hogwarts horror. Anne Robinson, you are fashion's Weakest Link!"

Barbra Streisand (1990): "What can I say? Yentl's gone mental." 1983: "A boy version of Medusa."

Bette Midler (1978): "She didn't go to a rummage sale, she wore it."

Camilla, Duchess of Cornwall (2001): "Packs the stylistic punch of a dilapidated Yorkshire pudding." 1995: "The Queen of Frump" and "the biggest bomb to hit Britain since the Blitz." 1994: "Her fashion image is way off track—she looked in the mirror and watched it crack."

Cher (1986): "*Popular Mechanics* Playmate of the Month. Someone must have thrown a monkey wrench into her fashion taste." 1984: "A plucked cockatoo setting femininity back twenty years."

David Bowie (1973): "A cross between Joan Crawford and Marlene Dietrich doing a glitter revival of New Faces."

Debbie Harry (1979): "Ten cents a dance with a nickel change."

Demi Moore (1989): "A Spandexed nightmare on Willis Street."

Dennis Rodman (1996): "The 'Fashion Menace' may be the Bad Boy of basketball, but in fishnet and feathers he's a unisex wreck."

Elizabeth Hurley (2000): "Her barely-there fashion bombs have hit a sour note—buy a coat."

Elton John (1975): "Would be the campiest spectacle in the Rose Parade."

Faye Dunaway (1991): "The Depressing Diva of Designer Dreck."

Geena Davis (1992): "Big Bird in heels."

Glenn Close (1992): "Dracula's Daughter."

Jane Seymour (1991): "A paisley peepshow on parade."

Jodie Foster (1991): "Her fashions would look better on Hannibal Lecter."

Julia Roberts (1992): "Hand out the hook for rag doll Roberts."

Kelly Osbourne (2002): "A fright-wigged baby doll stuck in a goth prom gown."

Madonna (1992): "The Bare-Bottomed Bore of Babylon." 1988: "Helpless, hopeless and horrendous."

Martha Stewart (1999): "Dresses like the centerfold for the *Farmer's Almanac*. She's a 3-D girl: dull, dowdy and devastatingly dreary. Definitely not 'a good thing.'"

Melanie Griffith (2003): "Melanie defines 'fatal fashion folly.' A botox'd cockatoo in a painting by Dalí!"

Paris Hilton (2003): "How are you gonna keep 'em down on the farm after they've seen Paree? Grab the blinders, here comes Paris. From cyber disgrace to red carpet chills—she's the vapid Venus of Beverly Hills!"

Roseanne (1989): "Bowling alley reject."

Sarah, Duchess of York (1996): "The bare-toed terror of London town. She looks like an unemployed barmaid in search of a crown." Also made the list in 1988 when she was accused of looking "like a horse that came in last." Blackwell went on to say "she looks terrible, like she should be making beds on the second floor of a motel."

Sinéad O'Connor (1992): "No tresses, no dresses. The high priestess of pretense downright depresses." 1990: "Nothing compares to the bald-headed banshee of MTV."

Queen Elizabeth II (1990): "God save the mothballs, the Stonehenge of style strikes again."

Tina Turner (1985): "Some women dress for men, some dress for women, some dress for laughs."

Renée Zellweger (2005): "A painted pumpkin on a pogo stick."

Yoko Ono (1972): "Oh no Yoko."

Nondrivers

Marianne Faithfull, Michael Jackson, David Copperfield, Claudia Schiffer, Anna Nicole Smith

N.B.: Albert Einstein never learned to drive.

People Who Changed Citizenship

Martina Navratilova (from Czech to American)

Nadia Comaneci (from Romanian to American)

Yehudi Menuhin (from American to British)

Greta Scacchi (from British to Australian)

Sheena Easton (from British to American)

Ivan Lendl (from Czech to American)

John Huston (from American to Irish)

T. S. Eliot (from American to British)

Josephine Baker (from American to French)

Jane Seymour (from British to American)

Anthony Hopkins (from British to American)

People Who Almost Never Give/Gave Interviews

Eric Clapton; Björn Borg; Peter Green; J. D. Salinger; Warren Beatty; Thomas Harris; Dan Aykroyd; Neil Armstrong; Kate Bush; Thomas Pynchon (has never even been photographed); Mutt Lange; John Deacon; Alan Rickman; David Lynch; Larry Mullen Jr.; David

Letterman; Syd Barrett; John Irving; Kate Moss; Chelsea Clinton; Camilla, Duchess of Cornwall; Harper Lee; J. J. Cale; Doris Day

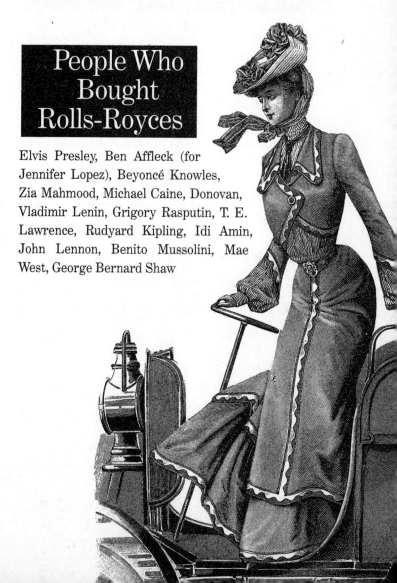

People Who Bought Rolls-Royces

Elvis Presley, Ben Affleck (for Jennifer Lopez), Beyoncé Knowles, Zia Mahmood, Michael Caine, Donovan, Vladimir Lenin, Grigory Rasputin, T. E. Lawrence, Rudyard Kipling, Idi Amin, John Lennon, Benito Mussolini, Mae West, George Bernard Shaw

People Who Own(ed)/ Co-own(ed) Restaurants

Alice Cooper: Cooperstown (Phoenix)

Jennifer Lopez: Madre's (Pasadena)

William Devane: Devane's (Palm Springs)

Wayne Gretzky: Wayne Gretzky's (Toronto)

Timothy Hutton: P. J. Clarke's (New York City)

Elton John: Le Dôme (Hollywood)

Ashton Kutcher: Dolce (Los Angeles)

Moby: TeaNY (New York City)

Jean-Paul Belmondo: Stressa (Paris)

Ricky Martin: Casa Salsa (Miami Beach)

Rob Schneider: Eleven (San Francisco)

Tom Selleck: The Black Orchid (Honolulu)

Sylvester Stallone, Bruce Willis and Arnold Schwarzenegger: the Planet Hollywood chain

Mariel Hemingway: Sam's Restaurant (Dallas)

Michael Caine: Langan's Brasserie (London)

Mikhail Baryshnikov: Columbus (New York City)

Robert De Niro, Bill Murray, Lou Diamond Phillips and Christopher Walken: TriBeCa Grill (New York City)

Bill Wyman: Sticky Fingers (London)

Patrick Swayze: Mulholland Drive Café (Los Angeles)

Dan Aykroyd: House of Blues restaurant/music-club chain

Whoopi Goldberg, Joe Pesci, Steven Seagal: Eclipse (Hollywood)

Steven Spielberg and Jeffrey Katzenberg: Dive! (Las Vegas)

Cameron Diaz: Bamboo (Miami)

Britney Spears: Nyla (New York City)

People Who Are Superstitious

Kylie Minogue, Engelbert Humperdinck, Elton John, Jelena Dokic, Mariah Carey, Jilly Cooper, Goran Ivanisevic

People Who Were Ordained Druids

William Blake, Winston Churchill, John Lennon

People and What They Collect

Patrick Stewart—*Beavis and Butt-Head* merchandise

George Michael (as a boy)—lizards and insects

Andre Agassi—Barry Manilow records

Clint Eastwood—jazz records

Helena Christensen—perfume bottles

Angelina Jolie—knives

Quentin Tarantino—old board games based on TV shows

Pink—stuffed frogs

Kevin Spacey—antique ashtrays

Jessica Biel—vintage eyeglasses without lenses

Dan Aykroyd—police badges

Beau Bridges—Native American percussion instruments

George W. Bush—autographed baseballs

J. C. Chasez—Hard Rock
Café menus

Bill Clinton—saxophones (real
ones and miniatures)

Stephen Dorff—vintage cameras

Patrick Duffy—antique toys and children's
books

Joey Fatone—Superman memorabilia

Larry Hagman—canes and flags

Mike Myers—model soldiers

Freddie Prinze Jr.—comic books

Noah Wyle—baseball cards

Jodie Foster—black-and-white photos

Sarah Michelle Gellar—rare books

Anna Kournikova—dolls from the countries she visits

Joan Rivers—Fabergé eggs

Roseanne—pigs

Meat Loaf—stuffed toys

Peter Jackson—World War I model airplanes

Rose McGowan—Marlene Dietrich memorabilia

Sports Stars Who've Appeared in Films

Sugar Ray Robinson—*Candy* (1968)

Muhammad Ali—*The Greatest* (1977)

Craig Stadler—*Tin Cup* (1996)

Ilie Nastase—*Players* (1979)

Magic Johnson—*Grand Canyon* (1991)

Pelé—*Hot Shot* (1987)

Michael Jordan—*Space Jam* (1996)

Vijay Amritraj—*Octopussy* (1983)

Ken Norton—*Mandingo* (1975)

Things Said About Books

"The man who doesn't read books has no advantage over the man that can't read them." (Mark Twain)

"The chief knowledge that a man gets from reading books is the knowledge that very few of them are worth reading." (H. L. Mencken)

"The oldest books are still only just out to those who have not read them." (Samuel Butler)

"**The books** that everybody admires are those that nobody reads." (Anatole France)

"**Books choose** their authors; the act of creation is not entirely a rational and conscious one." (Salman Rushdie)

"**The biggest** critics of my books are people who never read them." (Jackie Collins)

"**It is from books** that wise people derive consolation in the troubles of life." (Victor Hugo)

"**In the case** of good books, the point is not how many of them you can get through, but rather how many can get through to you." (Mortimer Adler)

"**All the known world,** excepting only savage nations, is governed by books." (Voltaire)

"**Books are divided** into two classes, the books of the hour and the books of all time." (John Ruskin)

"**Read the best** books first, or you may not have a chance to read them at all." (Henry David Thoreau)

"**To buy books** would be a good thing if we also could buy the time to read them." (Arthur Schopenhauer)

All the Winners of the Bulwer-Lytton Fiction Contest

Since 1982 the English department at San Jose State University has sponsored the Bulwer-Lytton Fiction Contest, a whimsical literary competition that challenges entrants to compose the opening sentence to the worst of all possible novels.

The camel died quite suddenly on the second day, and Selena fretted sulkily and, buffing her already impeccable nails—not for the first time since the journey began—pondered snidely if this would dissolve into a vignette of minor inconveniences like all the other holidays spent with Basil.

—Gail Cain, San Francisco, California (1983 winner)

The lovely woman-child Kaa was mercilessly chained to the cruel post of the warrior-chief Beast, with his barbarous tribe now stacking wood at her nubile feet, when the strong, clear voice of the poetic and heroic Handsomas roared, "Flick your Bic, crisp that chick, and you'll feel my steel through your last meal."

—Steven Garman, Pensacola, Florida (1984 winner)

The countdown had stalled at T minus 69 seconds when Desiree, the first female ape to go up in space, winked at me slyly and pouted her thick, rubbery lips unmistakably—the first of many such advances during what would

prove to be the longest, and most memorable, space voyage of my career.

—Martha Simpson, Glastonbury, Connecticut (1985 winner)

The bone-chilling scream split the warm summer night in two, the first half being before the scream when it was fairly balmy and calm and pleasant for those who hadn't heard the scream at all, but not calm or balmy or even very nice for those who did hear the scream, discounting the little period of time during the actual scream itself when your ears might have been hearing it but your brain wasn't reacting yet to let you know.

—Patricia E. Presutti, Lewiston, New York (1986 winner)

The notes blatted skyward as the sun rose over the Canada geese, feathered rumps mooning the day, webbed appendages frantically peddling unseen bicycles in their search for sustenance, driven by Nature's maxim, "Ya wanna eat, ya gotta work," and at last I knew Pittsburgh.

—Sheila B. Richter, Minneapolis, Minnesota (1987 winner)

Like an expensive sports car, fine-tuned and well built, Portia was sleek, shapely, and gorgeous, her red jumpsuit molding her body, which was as warm as the seatcovers in July, her hair as dark as new tires, her eyes flashing like bright hubcaps, and her lips as dewy as the beads of fresh rain on the hood; she was a woman driven—fueled by a single accelerant—and she needed a man, a man who wouldn't shift from his views, a man to steer her along the right road, a man like Alf Romeo.

—Rachel E. Sheeley, Williamsburg, Indiana (1988 winner)

Professor Frobisher couldn't believe he had missed seeing it for so long—it was, after all, right there under his nose—but in all his years of research into the intricate and mysterious ways of the universe, he had never noticed that the freckles on his upper lip, just below and to the left of the nostril, partially hidden until now by a hairy mole he had just removed a week before, exactly matched the pattern of the stars in the Pleides, down to the angry red zit that had just popped up where he and his colleagues had only today discovered an exploding nova.

—Ray C. Gainey, Indianapolis, Indiana (1989 winner)

Dolores breezed along the surface of her life like a flat stone forever skipping across smooth water, rippling reality sporadically but oblivious to it consistently, until she finally lost momentum, sank, and due to an overdose of fluoride as a child which caused her to lie forever on the floor of her life as useless as an appendix and as lonely as a five-hundred-pound barbell in a steroid-free fitness center.

—Linda Vernon, Newark, California (1990 winner)

Sultry it was and humid, but no whisper of air caused the plump, laden spears of golden grain to nod their burdened heads as they unheedingly awaited the cyclic rape of their gleaming treasure, while overhead the burning orb of luminescence ascended its ever-upward path toward a sweltering celestial apex, for although it is not in Kansas that our story takes place, it looks godawful like it.

—Judy Frazier, Lathrop, Missouri (1991 winner)

As the newest Lady Turnpot descended into the kitchen wrapped only in her celery-green dressing gown, her creamy bosom rising and falling like a temperamental soufflé, her tart mouth pursed in distaste, the sous-chef whispered to the scullery boy, "I don't know what to make of her."

—Laurel Fortuner, Montendre, France (1992 winner)

She wasn't really my type, a hard-looking but untalented reporter from the local cat box liner, but the first second that the third-rate representative of the fourth estate cracked open a new fifth of old Scotch, my sixth sense said seventh heaven was as close as an eighth note from Beethoven's Ninth Symphony, so, nervous as a tenth-grader drowning in eleventh-hour cramming for a physics exam, I swept her into my longing arms, and, humming "The Twelfth of Never," I got lucky on Friday the thirteenth.

—Wm. W. "Buddy" Ocheltree, Port Townsend, Washington (1993 winner)

97

As the fading light of a dying day filtered through the window blinds, Roger stood over his victim with a smoking .45, surprised at the serenity that filled him after pumping six slugs into the bloodless tyrant that mocked him day after day, and then he shuffled out of the office with one last look back at the shattered computer terminal lying there like a silicon armadillo left to rot on the information superhighway.
—Larry Brill, Austin, Texas (1994 winner)

Paul Revere had just discovered that someone in Boston was a spy for the British, and when he saw the young woman believed to be the spy's girlfriend in an Italian restaurant

he said to the waiter, "Hold the spumoni—I'm going to follow the chick an' catch a Tory."
—John L. Ashman, Houston, Texas (1995 winner)

"Ace, watch your head!" hissed Wanda urgently, yet somehow provocatively, through red, full, sensuous lips, but he couldn't, you know, since nobody can actually watch more than part of his nose or a little cheek or lips if he really tries, but he appreciated her warning.
—Janice Estey, Aspen, Colorado (1996 winner)

The moment he laid eyes on the lifeless body of the nude socialite sprawled across the bathroom floor, Detective Leary knew she had committed suicide by grasping the cap on the tamper-proof bottle, pushing down and twisting while she kept her thumb firmly pressed against the spot the arrow pointed to, until she hit the exact spot where the tab clicks into place, allowing her to remove the cap and swallow the entire contents of the bottle, thus ending her life.

—Artie Kalemeris, Fairfax, Virginia (1997 winner)

The corpse exuded the irresistible aroma of a piquant, ancho chili glaze enticingly enhanced with a hint of fresh cilantro as it lay before him, coyly garnished by a garland of variegated radicchio and caramelized onions, and impishly drizzled with glistening rivulets of vintage balsamic vinegar and roasted garlic oil; yes, as he surveyed the body of the slain food critic slumped on the floor of the cozy, but nearly empty, bistro, a quick inventory of his senses told corpulent Inspector Moreau that this was, in all likelihood, an inside job.

—Bob Perry, Milton, Massachusetts (1998 winner)

Through the gathering gloom of a late-October afternoon, along the greasy, cracked paving-stones slick from the sputum of the sky, Stanley Ruddlethorp wearily trudged up the hill from the cemetery where his wife, sister, brother, and three children were all buried, and forced open the door of his decaying house, blissfully unaware of the catastrophe that was soon to devastate his life.

—Dr. David Chuter, Kingston, Surrey, England (1999 winner)

The heather-encrusted Headlands, veiled in fog as thick as smoke in a crowded pub, hunched precariously over the moors, their rocky elbows slipping off land's end, their bulbous, craggy noses thrust into the thick foam of the North Sea like bearded old men falling asleep in their pints.
—Gary Dahl, Los Gatos, California (2000 winner)

A small assortment of astonishingly loud brass instruments raced each other lustily to the respective ends of their distinct musical choices as the gates flew open to release a torrent of tawny fur comprised of angry yapping bullets that nipped at Desdemona's ankles, causing her to reflect once again (as blood filled her sneakers and she fought her way through the panicking crowd) that the annual Running of the Pomeranians in Liechtenstein was a stupid idea.

—Sera Kirk, Vancouver, Canada (2001 winner)

On reflection, Angela perceived that her relationship with Tom had always been rocky, not quite a roller-coaster ride but more like when the toilet-paper roll gets a little squashed so it hangs crooked and every time you pull some off you can hear the rest going bumpity-bumpity in its holder until you go nuts and push it back into shape, a degree of annoyance that Angela had now almost attained.
—Rephah Berg, Oakland California (2002 winner)

They had but one last remaining night together, so they embraced each other as tightly as that two-flavor entwined string cheese that is orange and yellowish-white, the orange probably being a bland Cheddar and the white . . . Mozzarella, although it could possibly be Provolone or just plain American, as it really doesn't taste distinctly dissimilar from the orange, yet they would have you believe it does by coloring it differently.

—Mariann Simms, Wetumpka, Alabama (2003 winner)

She resolved to end the love affair with Ramon tonight . . . summarily, like Martha Stewart ripping the sand vein out of a shrimp's tail . . . though the term "love affair" now struck her as a ridiculous euphemism . . . not unlike "sand vein," which is after all an intestine, not a vein . . . and that tarry substance inside certainly isn't sand . . . and that brought her back to Ramon.

—Dave Zobel, Manhattan Beach, California (2004 winner)

As he stared at her ample bosom, he daydreamed of the dual Stromberg carburetors in his vintage Triumph Spitfire, highly functional yet pleasingly formed, perched prominently on top of the intake manifold, aching for experienced hands, the small knurled caps of the oil dampeners begging to be inspected and adjusted as described in chapter seven of the shop manual.

—Dan McKay, Fargo, North Dakota (2005 winner)

Fictional Characters and Their First Names

Dr. (John) Watson, Sherlock Holmes's sidekick

Mr. (Quincy) Magoo

Inspector (Jules) Maigret

(Wilfred) Ivanhoe

(Hugh) "Bulldog" Drummond

Little Lord (Cedric) Fauntleroy

Gilligan of Gilligan's Island had a first name that was used only once, on the never-aired pilot show: Willy

N.B.: Columbo's first name *isn't* Philip, despite claims that it is. His first name was never mentioned in the series.

Stupid Labels

On a packet of peanuts: "Warning: Contains nuts."

On a hair dryer: "Do not use while sleeping."

On a bar of Dial soap: "Directions: Use like regular soap."

On a tiramisu dessert (printed on bottom of box): "Do not turn upside down."

On a container of bread pudding: "Product will be hot after heating."

On packaging for a Rowenta iron: "Do not iron clothes on body."

On a bottle of children's cough medicine: "Do not drive a car or operate machinery after taking this medication."

On Nytol Sleep Aid: "Warning: May cause drowsiness."

On a set of Christmas lights: "For indoor or outdoor use only."

On a Japanese food processor: "Not to be used for the other use."

On a child's Superman costume: "Wearing of this garment does not enable you to fly."

On a Swedish chain saw: "Do not attempt to stop chain with your hands."

On a bottle of Palmolive dishwashing liquid: "Do not use on food."

Memorabilia Bought and Sold at Christie's

Dorothy's ruby slippers from *The Wizard of Oz:* $666,000 (2000)

Pelé's shirt from the 1958 World Cup Final: $125,000 (2004)

Marilyn Monroe's eternity ring (given to her by Joe DiMaggio after their 1954 wedding): $772,500 (1999)

Eric Clapton's 1956 Fender Stratocaster (as used on "Layla"): $497,500 (1999)

George Harrison's 1964 Gibson SG Standard guitar: $567,000 (2004)

John Lennon's handwritten lyrics to the Beatles song "Nowhere Man": $455,500 (2003)

An autographed life-size picture of Marlene Dietrich used in the famous crowd scene in Peter Blake's design for the Beatles' *Sgt. Pepper's Lonely Hearts Club Band* album cover: $152,500 (2003)

Britney Spears's primary school book report: $1,900 (2004)

James Bond's Aston Martin DB5: $280,000 (2001)

John Travolta's white suit from *Saturday Night Fever*: $145,500 (1995)

The Maltese Falcon icon from the 1941 film of the same name: $398,500 (1994)

The Rosebud sled from *Citizen Kane*: $233,500 (1996)

Clark Gable's personal script for *Gone With the Wind*: $244,500 (1996)

The dress Marilyn Monroe wore when she sang "Happy Birthday" to President John F. Kennedy at Madison Square Garden, New York, in 1962: $1,267,500 (1999)

Elvis Presley's 1942 Martin D-18 acoustic guitar: $175,000 (1993)

Bob Dylan's acoustic guitar from the 1960s: $20,000 (2004)

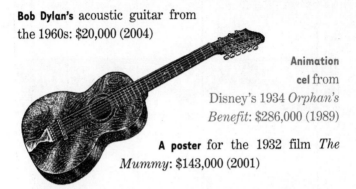

Animation cel from Disney's 1934 *Orphan's Benefit*: $286,000 (1989)

A poster for the 1932 film *The Mummy*: $143,000 (2001)

Celebrity Achievements

Sarah Michelle Gellar has a brown belt in tae kwon do.

Helen Mirren was named (British) Naturist (nudist) of the Year for 2004.

Of all his many talents, Leonardo da Vinci was proudest of his ability to bend iron with his bare hands.

Daryl Hannah invented a board game called Love It or Hate It.

Jeff Goldblum can wiggle his ears one at a time.

Benjamin Franklin invented bifocals so he could see two things at the same time.

Wynton Marsalis played trumpet with the New Orleans Philharmonic at the age of fourteen.

Michael Gambon, Bob Hoskins, Eric Bana and the late Art Carney all became successful actors without receiving any formal acting training.

People Who Are Proficient in Foreign Languages

Prince Philip (German)

Tim Roth (French and German)

Shirley MacLaine (Japanese)

Kylie Minogue (French)

Gloria Estefan (Spanish and French)

Sandra Bullock (German)

David Soul (German and Spanish)

Salma Hayek (Arabic)

Renée Zellweger (German)

Bill Clinton (German)

Stewart Copeland (Arabic)

Al Gore (Spanish)

William Shatner (French)

Montel Williams (Russian)

Kim Cattrall (German)

Geraldine Chaplin (Spanish)

Chelsea Clinton (German)

Jennifer Connelly (Italian and French)

Rebecca De Mornay (German and French)

Julie Dreyfus (Japanese)

Angie Everhart (French)

Molly Ringwald (French)

Sigourney Weaver (French and German)

J. K. Rowling (French)

Ashley Judd (French)

Alex Kingston (German)

Donna Summer (German)

Jodie Foster (French)

Christy Turlington (Spanish)

Ted Koppel (Russian, German and French)

Christopher Lee (German)

Lyle Lovett (German)

Dolph Lundgren (German, French and Japanese)

Bill Paxton (German)

Famke Janssen (German and French)

Rosamund Pike (German and French)

Greta Scacchi (German)

Nastassja Kinski (French, Italian and Russian)

Greg Kinnear (Greek)

Prince Michael of Kent (Russian)

Madeleine Albright (Russian)

Sting (Portuguese)

Orlando Bloom (French)

Condoleezza Rice (Russian)

People Who've Flown Helicopters

Sarah, Duchess of York; Prince Andrew; Prince Charles; Harrison Ford; Patricia Cornwell (bought a custom-painted Bell passenger helicopter, which she can legally fly alone, though she prefers to hire a copilot)

Awarded the Key of the City of . . .

Sean Connery (Edinburgh)

Sting (Newcastle)

Brigitte Bardot (Paris)

Jimmy Carter (Swansea)

Sarah, Duchess of York (York)

Nelson Mandela (Glasgow)

Richard Attenborough (Leicester)

Mikhail Gorbachev (Aberdeen)

Paul McCartney (Liverpool)

Bill Clinton (Dublin)

Margaret Thatcher (Westminster)

Prince Charles (Swansea)

Cliff Richard (London)

People Who Had Airports Named After Them

John Wayne (Santa Ana)

John F. Kennedy (New York)

Charles de Gaulle (Paris)

David Ben-Gurion (Tel Aviv)

Leonardo da Vinci (Rome)

Chiang Kai-shek (Taipei)

Pierre Trudeau (Montreal)

Jan Smuts (Johannesburg)

Pope John Paul II (Krakow)

Antoine de Saint-Exupéry (Lyon)

Marco Polo (Venice)

Jomo Kenyatta (Nairobi)

Pablo Picasso (Málaga)

Konrad Adenauer (Cologne)

John Lennon (Liverpool)

Chuck Yeager (Charleston)

George Bush (Houston)

Louis Armstrong (New Orleans)

Will Rogers (Oklahoma City)

Wolfgang Mozart (Salzburg)

People Who've Had Theaters Named After Them

Bob Hope (Eltham, U.K.)

John Gielgud (London, U.K.)

Peggy Ashcroft (Croydon, U.K.)

Neil Simon (New York)

Michael Redgrave (Farnham, U.K.)

Laurence Olivier (London, U.K.)

Tony O'Reilly (Pittsburgh)

Flora Robson (Newark, U.K.)

Named
"Sexiest Man Alive"
by *People* Magazine

Matthew McConaughey (2005)

Jude Law (2004)

Johnny Depp (2003)

Ben Affleck (2002)

Pierce Brosnan (2001)

Brad Pitt (2000)

Richard Gere (1999)

Harrison Ford (1998)

George Clooney (1997)

Denzel Washington (1996)

Brad Pitt (1995)

111

Richard Gere and Cindy Crawford (in 1993 they
were named "The Sexiest Couple
Alive"—in 1994 there was no award)

Nick Nolte (1992)

Patrick Swayze (1991)

Tom Cruise (1990)

Sean Connery (1989)

John F. Kennedy Jr. (1988)

Harry Hamlin (1987)

Mark Harmon (1986)

Mel Gibson (1985)

People Honored with Ticker-Tape Parades in New York City

Charles Lindbergh (June 13, 1927)

David Lloyd George (October 5, 1923)

Bobby Jones (July 2, 1926, and July 2, 1930)

Ramsay MacDonald (October 4, 1929)

Amelia Earhart (June 20, 1932)

Howard Hughes (July 15, 1938)

Dwight Eisenhower (June 10, 1945)

Charles de Gaulle (August 27, 1945, and April 26, 1960)

Winston Churchill (March 14, 1946)

Eamon de Valera (March 9, 1948)

Jawaharlal Nehru (October 17, 1949)

Liaquat Ali Khan (May 8, 1950)

Robert Menzies (August 4, 1950)

Douglas MacArthur (April 20, 1951)

David Ben-Gurion (May 9, 1951)

Ben Hogan (July 21, 1953)

Haile Selassie (June 1, 1954, and October 4, 1963)

Althea Gibson (July 11, 1957)

Queen Elizabeth II (October 21, 1957)

Willy Brandt (February 10, 1959)

John F. Kennedy (October 19, 1960)

John Glenn (March 1, 1962)

Pope John Paul II (October 3, 1979)

Nelson Mandela (June 20, 1990)

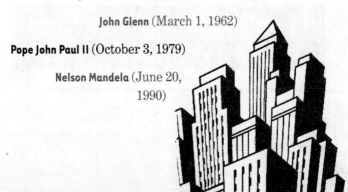

People Who've Launched Products

Muhammad Ali—sportswear

Sean "P. Diddy" Combs—Sean John, a "tightly edited collection" of clothing

MC Hammer—a clothing line called the J. Slick Collection

Catherine Zeta-Jones—babywear

John Malkovich—a clothing line called Mrs. Mudd

Hilary Duff—a line of canine clothing called Little Dog Duff

Madonna—a clothing line called the English Roses Collection

Bono—Edun ("nude" spelled backward), socially conscious apparel

Gwen Stefani—a fashion label named L.A.M.B.

People Who've Launched Perfumes

Céline Dion—Belong

Stella McCartney—Stella

Paloma Picasso—Paloma Picasso

Cliff Richard—Miss You Nights

Britney Spears—Curious

Paris Hilton—Paris Hilton

Jennifer Lopez—Miami Glow

Antonio Banderas—Spirit

Old Scottish Proverbs

"What may be done at any time will be done at no time."

"False friends are worse than bitter enemies."

"Fools look to tomorrow; wise men use tonight."

"They talk of my drinking but never my thirst."

"The day has eyes, the night has ears."

"One may survive distress, but not disgrace."

"Perfect love cannot be without equality."

"Here's to you, as good as you are, and here's to me, as bad as I am. But as good as you are, and as bad as I am, I am as good as you are, as bad as I am."

115

"**Danger and delight** grow on one stalk."

"**Were it not** for hope, the heart would break."

"**Forsake not God** till you find a better master."

"**Money is flat** and meant to be piled up."

"**It's a sad house** where the hen crows louder than the cock."

"**Never marry** for money. Ye'll borrow it cheaper."

"**Be happy** while you're living, for you're a long time dead."

Astronomy

A day on Jupiter is approximately 9 hours, 50 minutes and 30 seconds at the equator.

Average wind speed on Jupiter is 225 miles per hour.

The volume of the Moon and the volume of the Pacific Ocean are the same.

Most stars shine for at least 10 billion years.

The Earth is the densest planet in the solar system.

It takes 8 minutes and 12 seconds for sunlight to reach Earth.

A manned rocket reaches the Moon in less time than it once took a stagecoach to travel the length of England.

The British comic legend Will Hay was an expert astronomer, who discovered the spot on the planet Saturn in 1933.

The winds on Saturn blow at 1,200 miles per hour—10 times faster than a strong Earth hurricane.

The number of UFO sightings increases when Mars is nearest Earth.

Every 11 years the magnetic poles of the Sun switch, in a cycle called solar maximum.

Astronauts can't burp in space: there's no gravity to separate liquid from gas in their stomachs.

While astronauts might feel upset in space, lack of gravity will prevent tears from rolling down their face.

For every extra kilogram carried on a space flight, 530 kilograms of excess fuel is needed at liftoff.

Eggs

The tradition of decorating eggs at Easter started thousands of years ago to celebrate the return of spring after a hard winter. Eggs symbolize new life.

In Basel, Switzerland, in 1471, a cockerel was found guilty in a court of law for laying an egg "in defiance of natural law." The bird was then burned at the stake as a "devil in disguise."

You can tell an egg is fresh if it sinks to the bottom of a pan of water. Eggs take in air as they age, so an old egg floats more easily.

Crushed eggshells sprinkled around lettuce plants should help to stop insects from nibbling the leaves.

In peak production, hens lay one egg a day.

In parts of France, brides break an egg for luck before they enter their new home.

Paul Newman's character in *Cool Hand Luke* eats fifty hard-boiled eggs.

Writers Who've Had a Manuscript Lost or Stolen

Louis de Bernières (the first fifty pages of *A Partisan's Daughter*)

Malcolm Lowry

Thomas Wolfe (*Mannerhouse*—rewrote it entirely)

T. E. Lawrence (*The Seven Pillars of Wisdom*—rewrote it in full after losing it while changing trains at Reading station in 1919)

John Steinbeck (*Of Mice and Men*—the first draft was eaten by his dog)

Jilly Cooper (*Riders*, her first big blockbuster book—
she lost the first draft)

People Who Wrote Just One Novel

Anna Sewell: *Black Beauty*

Margaret Mitchell: *Gone With the Wind*

Harper Lee: *To Kill a Mockingbird*

Emily Brontë: *Wuthering Heights*

Kenneth Grahame: *The Wind in the Willows*

People (more famous for other things) Who've Written Works of Fiction

Robert Shaw (*The Sun Doctor*)

Sarah Bernhardt (*In the Clouds*)

George Kennedy (*Murder on Location*)

Jean Harlow (*Today Is Tonight*)

Joan Collins (*Prime Time*)

Leslie Caron (*Vengeance*)

119

Mae West (*The Constant Sinner*)

Naomi Campbell (*Swan*)

Benito Mussolini (*The Cardinal's Mistress*)

Julie Andrews (*The Last of the Really Great Whangdoodles*)

Martina Navratilova (*Total Zone*)

Winston Churchill (*Savrola*)

Carly Simon (*Amy the Dancing Bear*)

Tony Curtis (*Kid Andrew Cody and Julie Sparrow*)

Whoopi Goldberg (*Alice*)

Jane Seymour (*This One and That One*)

Michael Palin (*Small Harry and the Toothache Pills*)

Ethan Hawke (*The Hottest State*)

Johnny Cash (*Man in White*)

Shakespeare's Longest Roles

Falstaff (1,614 lines in *Henry IV, Parts 1 & 2* and *The Merry Wives of Windsor*)

Hamlet (1,422 lines in *Hamlet*—making Hamlet the longest role in any *single* Shakespeare play)

Richard III (1,124 lines in *Richard III*)

Iago (1,097 lines in *Othello*)

Henry V (1,025 lines in *Henry V*)

Othello (860 lines in *Othello*)

Vincentio (820 lines in *Measure for Measure*)

Coriolanus (809 lines in *Coriolanus*)

Timon (795 lines in *Timon of Athens*)

Marc Antony (766 lines in *Antony and Cleopatra*)

Things Said About Poetry

"Poetry is the lava of the imagination whose eruption prevents an earthquake." (Lord Byron)

"Poetry is what gets lost in translation." (Robert Frost)

"Poetry is living proof that rhyme doesn't pay." (Anonymous)

"There's no money in poetry, but there's no poetry in money, either." (Robert Graves)

"A poet in history is divine; but a poet in the next room is a joke." (Max Eastman)

"**Poetry** is an evasion of the real job of writing prose."
(Sylvia Plath)

"**Poetry** often enters through the window of irrelevance."
(M. C. Richards)

"**Genuine** poetry can communicate before it is
understood." (T. S. Eliot)

"**Most** people ignore most poetry because most poetry
ignores most people." (Adrian Mitchell)

"**Poetry** is the language in which man explores his
own amazement." (Christopher Fry)

"**Any healthy man** can go without food for two days—but not
without poetry." (Charles Baudelaire)

"**Poetry** comes nearer to vital truth than history."
(Plato)

People and the Approximate Value of Their Autographs

Adolf Hitler: $10,300

Marilyn Monroe: $8,600

Winston Churchill: $8,600

Harry Houdini: $6,900

Albert Einstein: $6,900

Horatio Nelson: $6,900

Bruce Lee: $6,900

John F. Kennedy: $6,000

Diana, Princess of Wales: $6,000

Oscar Wilde: $5,600

Napoleon: $5,150

John Lennon: $5,150

Charles Dickens: $5,150

Alfred Hitchcock: $5,150

Pablo Picasso: $5,150

Elvis Presley: $4,300

Jimi Hendrix: $3,400

Cary Grant: $3,400

Judy Garland: $3,400

Bob Marley: $3,400

Yuri Gagarin: $2,600

Buddy Holly: $2,600

Grace Kelly: $2,150

Andy Warhol: $1,700

Walt Disney: $1,700

Mother Teresa: $1,500

Errol Flynn: $1,300

River Phoenix: $1,300

Queen Victoria: $1,000

James Cagney: $1,000

Salvador Dalí: $800

Things That Began in the 1960s

Jiffy bags, aluminum kitchen foil, discotheques, flavored potato chips, running shoes, hatchbacks, self-service gas stations, fruit-flavored yogurts, pocket calculators, felt-tip pens, Weight Watchers, color TV, long-life milk, electric toothbrushes, the contraceptive pill, safety belts, Brut 33, the miniskirt, James Bond films, Ibuprofen, *Peanuts*, Twister, Pringles, Saran Wrap, the Jacuzzi, bar codes

Things That Began in the 1970s

Bell-bottoms, lava lamps, the CD, *Scooby-Doo*, soft contact lenses, punk music, floppy disks, the VCR, Post-its, lipo-suction, word processors, gay lib, hot pants, genetic engineering, test-tube babies, palimony

The Way We Live

The average person spends 2 weeks over a lifetime waiting for the traffic lights to change.

One in 10 people live on an island.

Married men change their underwear twice as often as single men.

Every year a ton of cement is poured for every man, woman and child in the world.

If you are struck by lightning once, you are 100,000 times more likely to get struck another time than is someone who has never been struck.

It is said that small particles of fecal matter can become airborne during toilet flushing, and dentists recommend keeping your toothbrush 6 feet away from the toilet to avoid contamination. If your bathroom isn't big enough, put the lid down before flushing.

Sixty-two percent of e-mail is spam.

After hours working at a computer display, look at a blank piece of white paper. It will probably appear pink.

There is no such thing as naturally blue food—blueberries are purple.

The QWERTY typewriter was designed so that the left hand would type the most common letters—it was a means of slowing down typists and keeping the typewriters from jamming.

Fingerprints provide traction for the fingers.

Experts in the paranormal say we reach the peak of our ability to see ghosts at the age of seven.

Laughing lowers levels of stress hormones and strengthens the immune system.

Women burn fat more slowly than men.

Only a third of the people who can twitch their ears can twitch them one at a time.

During menstruation the sensitivity of a woman's middle finger is reduced.

Seventy-one percent of office workers stopped on the street for a survey agreed to give up their computer passwords in exchange for a chocolate bar.

Amusement park attendance goes up after a fatal accident. It seems that people want to take the same ride that killed someone.

Sixty-four percent of people can roll their tongue.

Most toilets flush in E-flat.

Drivers tend to go faster when other cars are around. It doesn't matter where the other cars are—whether in front, behind or alongside.

Most digital alarm clocks ring in the key of B-flat.

In the average lifetime, a person will walk the equivalent of 5 times around the equator.

Wearing headphones for an hour increases the bacteria in your ear by 700 times.

A computer user blinks on average 7 times a minute.

If you gave each human on Earth an equal portion of dry land, including the uninhabitable areas, everyone would get roughly 100 square feet.

During a lifetime the average person drinks 8,000 gallons of water and uses 68,250 gallons of water to brush his or her teeth.

The average person flexes the joints in his or her fingers 24 million times in a lifetime.

There's a systematic lull in conversation every 7 minutes.

We forget 80 percent of what we learn every day.

Fifty percent of lingerie purchases are returned to the shop.

The average smell weighs 760 nanograms.

There are 4.3 births and 1.7 deaths in the world every second.

If we had the same mortality rate now as in 1900, more than half the people in the world today would be dead.

If all the chocolate Easter eggs sold in Britain in one year were laid end to end, they'd go from London to Australia and halfway back again.

Women shoplift more often than men.

A baby balances on two feet and an arm when it crawls.

The original purpose of the tablecloth was as a towel on which to wipe fingers and hands after eating.

The melting point of cocoa butter is just below body temperature—and that's why chocolate literally melts in your mouth.

Smelling bananas and/or green apples can help you lose weight.

Women speak an average of 7,000 words a day, men, an average of just over 2,000.

Stores have found that the color purple makes people feel like spending money.

Honey

The honeybee is the only insect that produces food eaten by humans.

Historically honey was used to treat cuts and burns.

The Romans used honey instead of gold to pay their taxes.

Honey was part of Cleopatra's daily beauty ritual.

Beehives were sometimes used in ancient warfare, lobbed at the enemy as a kind of bomb.

It takes the nectar from 2 million flowers to make a pound of honey. One bee would therefore have to fly about 90,000 miles—three times around the globe—to make a pound of honey.

A bee visits 50 to 100 flowers during a collection trip and makes altogether about a twelfth of a teaspoon of honey during its life.

The buzz of a honeybee comes from its wings, which beat more than 11,000 times a minute.

Worker bees are all female.

Honeybees have hair on their eyes.

An explorer who found a 2,000-year-old jar of honey in an Egyptian tomb said it tasted delicious.

Bees use the shortest route possible to reach the flower of their choice, hence the expression "making a beeline for something."

Science

Copper exposed to arsenic turns black.

The cracks in breaking glass move at speeds up to 3,000 miles per hour.

A whip "cracks" because its tip moves faster than the speed of sound.

Water freezes faster if it starts from a warm temperature than a cool one.

René Descartes came up with the theory of coordinate geometry by watching a fly walk across a ceiling.

Sound travels 15 times faster through steel than through air.

Methane gas can often be seen bubbling up in ponds. It is produced by decomposing plants and animals in the mud at the bottom.

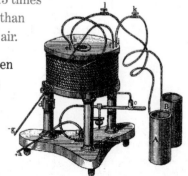

An ounce of gold can be beaten into a thin film covering 100 square feet.

Lightning strikes our planet about 6,000 times a minute.

It is harder to reach the speed of sound at sea level than at altitude.

The silvery metal gallium is liquid at 85.6 degrees Fahrenheit, which means it would melt in your hand. Cesium is another metal that would melt in your hand, but it would also react violently with your skin and possibly catch fire. The third metal that is liquid at more or less room temperature is mercury.

If you went unprotected into space, you would explode before you suffocated.

The holes in flyswatters are there to reduce air resistance. For the same reason, you should open your fingers when trying to kill mosquitoes by hand (it works).

Every megabyte sent over the Internet needs two lumps of coal to power it.

A car traveling at 50 miles per hour needs half of its fuel just to overcome wind resistance.

The liquid inside young coconuts can be used as a substitute for blood plasma.

It takes 4,000 crocuses to produce a single ounce of saffron.

Pure gold is so soft that it can be molded with the hands (which is why they add copper to 24-karat gold).

Because of the Earth's gravity, it's impossible for mountains to be taller than 9 miles.

Plants don't necessarily look like their "parents," but they always look like their "grandparents."

If you think of the Milky Way as being the size of Asia, then our solar system would be the size of a penny.

Bone China is so called because powdered animal bone is mixed with the clay to make it white and translucent.

There are 20,000 living organisms in a glass of water.

Every diamond, no matter how big, is just a single molecule.

Music

Johnny Depp played guitar on "Fade In-Out" by Oasis and appeared in the video for Tom Petty's "Into the Wide Great Open."

John Cage composed *Imaginary Landscape No. 4,*

which was scored for twelve radios tuned at random.

Karen Carpenter's doorbell chimed the first six notes of "We've Only Just Begun."

Actor Jon Voight's brother, Chip Taylor, wrote the song "Wild Thing."

Songs That Don't Feature Their Titles in the Lyrics

"A Day In The Life" (The Beatles)

"Ballad of John and Yoko" (The Beatles)

"For You Blue" (The Beatles)

"Tomorrow Never Knows" (The Beatles)

"Ambulance" (Blur)

"Space Oddity" (David Bowie)

"For What It's Worth" (Buffalo Springfield)

"Superstar" (The Carpenters)

"Death of a Ladies' Man" (Leonard Cohen)

"The Scientist" (Coldplay)

"Badge" (Cream)

"Suite: Judy Blue Eyes" (Crosby, Stills and Nash)

"7 Days" (Craig David)

"Annie's Song" (John Denver)

"It Takes a Lot to Laugh, It Takes a Train to Cry" (Bob Dylan)

"Positively 4th Street" (Bob Dylan)

"Subterranean Homesick Blues" (Bob Dylan)

"Guilty Conscience" (Eminem)

"The Circus" (Erasure)

"Earth Song" (Michael Jackson)

"Black Dog" (Led Zeppelin)

"The Battle of Evermore" (Led Zeppelin)

"#9 Dream" (John Lennon)

"Act of Contrition" (Madonna)

"Creeque Alley" (The Mamas and the Papas)

"Porcelain" (Moby)

"Alternate Title" (The Monkees—the original title, which they were obliged to drop, was "Randy Scouse Git," which also didn't feature in the lyrics)

"Hate This and I'll Love You" (Muse)

"Smells Like Teen Spirit" (Nirvana)

"Shakermaker" (Oasis)

"Brain Damage" (Pink Floyd)

"American Trilogy" (Elvis Presley)

"Bohemian Rhapsody" (Queen—although it did contain the title of the song that knocked it off the top of the British charts—ABBA's "Mamma Mia")

"Talk Show Host" (Radiohead)

"Endless Cycle" (Lou Reed)

"The Sidewinder Sleeps Tonight" (R.E.M.)

"The Millennium Prayer" (Cliff Richard)

"Unchained Melody" (The Righteous Brothers)

"Sympathy for the Devil" (The Rolling Stones)

"Pyjamarama" (Roxy Music)

"The Immigrant Song" (Neil Sedaka)

"For Emily, Whenever I May Find Her" (Simon and Garfunkel)

"Pretzel Logic" (Steely Dan)

"The Caves of Altamira" (Steely Dan)

"Father and Son" (Cat Stevens)

"Richard III" (Supergrass)

"The Logical Song" (Supertramp)

"The Unforgettable Fire" (U2)

"Tom's Diner" (Suzanne Vega)

Songs with False Endings

"Light My Fire" (The Doors)

"Good Vibrations" (The Beach Boys)

"I Got You Babe" (Sonny and Cher)

"Monday Monday" (The Mamas and the Papas)

"Strawberry Fields Forever" (The Beatles)

"In the Mood" (Glenn Miller)

"The Twist" (Chubby Checker)

"Visions" (Stevie Wonder)

"All by Myself" (Eric Carmen)

"The Best Part of Breaking Up" (The Ronettes)

Songs That Were #1 on Both Sides of the Atlantic at the Same Time

"I Just Called to Say I Love You" (Stevie Wonder: October 13–20, 1984)

"I Feel Fine" (The Beatles: December 26 1964–January 14, 1965)

"Maggie May" (Rod Stewart: October 9–November 6, 1971)

"Honky Tonk Woman" (The Rolling Stones: August 23–30, 1969)

"Without You" (Nilsson: March 11–18, 1972)

"I Will Survive" (Gloria Gaynor: March 17–24, 1979)

"(Everything I Do) I Do It for You" (Bryan Adams: July 27–September 14, 1991)

"Billie Jean" (Michael Jackson: March 5–12, 1983)

"Bridge Over Troubled Water" (Simon and Garfunkel: March 28–April 11, 1970)

"Night Fever" (The Bee Gees: April 29–May 13, 1978)

People Who Are—or Used to Be—in Pop Groups

Bruce Willis was in the band Loose Goose.

Woody Harrelson is lead singer in the band Manly Moondog and the Three Kool Hats.

River Phoenix was the vocalist in Aleka's Attic.

Instruments and the People Who Play Them

Bass guitar (Gary Sinise)

Guitar (Paul Bettany)

Piano and cello (Rosamund Pike)

French horn and trumpet (Samuel L. Jackson)

Guitar (Minnie Driver)

Harmonica (Dan Aykroyd)

Banjo (Steve Martin)

Piano (Jeff Goldblum)

Guitar (Kate Hudson)

Violin (Meryl Streep)

Guitar (Ricky Gervais)

Guitar (Paris Hilton)

The Beatles by Number

Note that some numbers appear in more than one song.

½ "Yesterday"

1 "Day Tripper"

2 "Two of Us"

3 "Come Together"

4 "You Never Give Me Your Money"

5 "She's Leaving Home"

6 "All Together Now"

7 "And Your Bird Can Sing"

8 "Eight Days a Week"

9 "Revolution 9"

10 "Being for the Benefit of Mr. Kite"

12 "Cry Baby Cry"

15 "She Came in Through the Bathroom Window"

17 "I Saw Her Standing There"

19 "Taxman"

20 "Sgt. Pepper's Lonely Hearts Club Band"

31 "Maxwell's Silver Hammer"

50 "Maxwell's Silver Hammer"

64 "When I'm 64"

909 "One After 909"

1,000 "Paperback Writer" or "The Fool on the Hill"

4,000 "A Day in the Life"

1,000,000 "Across the Universe"

Around the World in Beatles Songs

Amsterdam "The Ballad of John and Yoko"

Bishopsgate "Being for the Benefit of Mr. Kite"

Blackburn, Lancashire "A Day in the Life"

California "Get Back"

Dakota "Rocky Raccoon"

France "The Ballad of John and Yoko"

Georgia "Back in the USSR"

Gibraltar "The Ballad of John and Yoko"

Holland "The Ballad of John and Yoko"

Isle of Wight "When I'm 64"

Lime Street "Maggie Mae"

Liverpool "Maggie Mae"

London "The Ballad of John and Yoko"

L.A. "Blue Jay Way"

Miami Beach "Back in the USSR"

Moscow "Back in the USSR"

Paris "The Ballad of John and Yoko"

Penny Lane "Penny Lane"

Southampton "The Ballad of John and Yoko"

Spain "The Ballad of John and Yoko"

Tucson, Arizona "Get Back"

Ukraine "Back in the USSR"

Vienna "The Ballad of John and Yoko"

Just Some of the Beatles Tribute Bands

The Bootleg Beatles

Cavern

All You Need Is Love

Apple

The Backbeat Beatles

The Brazilian Beetles

Come Together

The Eggmen

The Fake Beatles

The Upbeat Beatles

The Fab Beatles

The Beatels

Revolver

Backbeat

Day Tripper

Day Trippers

The Fab Walrus

Help!

The Imagine

The Moptops

Rain

The Fab Four

The Beatleg

Apple Pies

Shout!

Strawberry Fields

Yesterday

Celebrities and the Records They Released

Patrick Swayze: "Raisin' Heaven and Hell Tonight"

David Copperfield: "Summer Days"

Farrah Fawcett: "You"

Elizabeth Taylor: "Wings in the Sky"

Clint Eastwood: "I Talk to the Trees"

Leonard Nimoy: "Proud Mary"

William Shatner: "Mr. Tambourine Man"

Lon Chaney Jr.: "Monster Holiday"

143

Diego Maradona: "La Mano de Dios" (The Hand of God)

Russell Crowe: "I Want to Be Like Marlon Brando"

Billy Crystal: "The Christmas Song"

Meryl Streep: "Amazing Grace"

Peter Fonda: "Catch the Wind"

Linda Evans: "Don't You Need"

Britt Ekland: "Do It to Me"

Anthony Hopkins: "A Distant Star"

Oliver Reed: "Lonely for a Girl"

Rebecca De Mornay: "Oh Jimmy"

Gene Wilder: "Pure Imagination"

Raquel Welch: "This Girl's Back in Town"

Burt Reynolds: "I Like Having You Around"

Robert Mitchum: "Ballad of Thunder Road"

Princess Stephanie of Monaco: "Live Your Life"

Ingrid Bergman: "This Old Man"

Richard Chamberlain: "Love Me Tender"

The First Videos Ever Shown on MTV (1981)

"Video Killed the Radio Star" (The Buggles)

"You Better Run" (Pat Benatar)

"She Won't Dance with Me" (Rod Stewart)

"You Better You Bet" (The Who)

"Little Susie's on the Up" (PhD)

"We Don't Talk Anymore" (Cliff Richard)

"Brass in Pocket" (The Pretenders)

"Time Heals" (Todd Rundgren)

"Take It on the Run" (REO Speedwagon)

"Rockin' the Paradise" (Styx)

People Who've Had Songs Written for Them

Woody Harrelson—"Woody" (Hootie and the Blowfish)

Gwyneth Paltrow—"Moses" (Chris Martin)

Angie Bowie—"Angie" (The Rolling Stones)

Carole King—"Oh! Carol" (Neil Sedaka)

Patti D'Arbanville—"Lady D'Arbanville" (Cat Stevens)

Rosanna Arquette—"Rosanna" (Toto)

Diana, Princess of Wales—"Candle in the Wind 1997" (Elton John)

Magic Johnson—"Positive" (Michael Franti)

David Geffen—"A Free Man in Paris" (Joni Mitchell)

Eric Clapton—"My Favorite Mistake" (Sheryl Crow)

Robert F. Kennedy—"Long Time Gone" (David Crosby)

Syd Barrett—"Shine on You Crazy Diamond" (Roger Waters)

Duke Ellington—"Sir Duke" (Stevie Wonder)

Kari-Anne Jagger (wife of Chris Jagger)—"Carrie Anne" (The Hollies)

Meteorology

It would take 7 billion particles of fog to fill a teaspoon. A cubic mile of fog is made up of less than a gallon of water.

The sunlight that strikes the Earth at any given moment (in total) weighs as much as a large ocean liner.

A snowflake can take up to an hour to land.

Twelve percent of the Earth's land surface is permanently covered by ice and snow.

The South Pole has no sun for 182 days each year.

> **On July 17, 1841,** a shower of hail and rain in Derby, U.K., was accompanied by a cascade of hundreds of small fish and frogs—some of them still alive.

Small clouds that look like they have broken off from bigger clouds are called scuds.

> **A full Moon** always rises at sunset.

A full Moon is nine times brighter than a half Moon.

> **On August 14, 1979,** a rainbow over North Wales lasted for three hours.

People Who've Appeared in Soap Operas

Christian Slater—*Ryan's Hope*

Ricky Martin—*General Hospital*; started as a singing bartender and then got a regular role

Russell Crowe—*Neighbors*

Val Kilmer—*Knots Landing*

Ben Kingsley—*Coronation Street*

Brad Pitt—*Dallas*

Jude Law—*Families*

Demi Moore—*General Hospital*

Kevin Kline—*Search for Tomorrow*

Alec Baldwin—*The Doctors*

Tommy Lee Jones—*One Life to Live*

Morgan Freeman—*Another World*

Kevin Bacon—*The Guiding Light*

Meg Ryan—*As the World Turns*

Davy Jones—*Coronation Street*

Christopher Walken—*The Guiding Light*

Marisa Tomei—*As the World Turns*

Sigourney Weaver—*Somerset*

Ian McKellen—*Coronation Street*

Ray Liotta—*Another World*

Susan Sarandon—*Search for Tomorrow*

People Who've Made Guest Appearances on TV Shows

Richard Branson—*Baywatch*

Paul McCartney—*Baywatch*

Leonard Cohen—*Miami Vice*

Ray Charles—*Moonlighting*

Stevie Wonder—*The Cosby Show*

Peter Noone—*My Two Dads*

Phil Collins—*Miami Vice*

Frank Sinatra—*Magnum, P.I.*

Dionne Warwick—*The Rockford Files*

Carly Simon—*thirtysomething*

Boy George—*The A-Team*

Davy Jones—*My Two Dads*

Ewan McGregor—*ER*

TV Shows That Started as Radio Shows

What's My Line?

This Is Your Life

Dragnet

Perry Mason

Gunsmoke

The Lone Ranger

Films That Became TV Series

Young Dr. Kildare

Casablanca

In the Heat of the Night

The Third Man

The Saint

Sitcoms That Were Spin-Offs from Other Sitcoms

Frasier *(Cheers)*

Empty Nest *(The Golden Girls)*

Laverne and Shirley *(Happy Days)*

Rhoda *(The Mary Tyler Moore Show)*

Phyllis *(The Mary Tyler Moore Show)*

Lou Grant *(The Mary Tyler Moore Show)*

Tabitha *(Bewitched)*

Joey *(Friends)*

Joanie Loves Chachi *(Happy Days)*

Mork and Mindy *(Laverne and Shirley)*

Flo *(Alice)*

The Jeffersons *(All in the Family)*

Petticoat Junction *(The Beverly Hillbillies)*

A Different World *(The Cosby Show)*

Benson *(Soap)*

Ally *(Ally McBeal)*

Dogs

The average life span of a dog is between 8 and 15 years, depending on the breed.

The largest amount of money left to a dog was $25.9 million—to a poodle in 1931 by one Ella Wendel of New York.

Dogs can distinguish between nonidentical twins by smell—but they can't distinguish between identical twins.

Queen Elizabeth II is the world's most famous owner of corgis. The names she's given to her dogs include Fable, Myth, Shadow, Jolly and Chipper.

The breeds that bite the most are German shepherds, chows and poodles.

The breeds that bite the least are golden retrievers, Labradors and Old English sheepdogs.

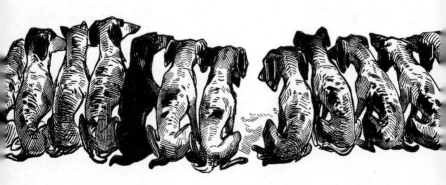

As a result of inbreeding, three out of every ten Dalmatians suffer from a hearing disability.

Dogs don't need to eat citrus fruit because they make their own vitamin C.

People who used to sleep with their dog in the bed next to them include the Duke of Windsor, General Custer and Elizabeth Barrett Browning.

In Japan, they sell toupees for dogs.

Thirty-three percent of U.S. dog owners admit that they talk to their dog on the phone.

Dogs can be trained to smell the presence of autism in children, while "seizure alert" dogs are able to alert their owners before the onset of an epileptic seizure. Dogs can also predict diabetic coma and detect certain cancers.

At the end of World War I, the German government trained the first guide dogs to assist blind war veterans.

The most intelligent dog breeds are (in order): border collie, poodle, German shepherd, and golden retriever.

Dogs on film: *Beethoven, The Fox and the Hound, 101 Dalmatians, K-9, Lady and the Tramp, Oliver & Company, Turner & Hooch* (but not *Reservoir Dogs*).

Dogs in literature: Nana in *Peter Pan* by J. M. Barrie; Toto in *The Wizard of Oz* by Frank Baum; Timmy in *The Famous Five* books by Enid Blyton; Edison in *Chitty Chitty Bang Bang* by Ian Fleming; Montmorency in *Three Men in a Boat* by Jerome K. Jerome; Bullseye in *Oliver Twist* by Charles Dickens; Jip in *Dr. Dolittle* by Hugh Lofting; Argos in *The Odyssey* by Homer; Old Yeller in *Old Yeller* by Fred Gipson; Lassie in the books, movies, and shows by various writers.

"A dog teaches a boy fidelity, perseverance and to turn around three times before lying down." (Robert Benchley)

"I loathe people who keep dogs. They are cowards who haven't got the guts to bite people themselves." (August Strindberg)

"That indefatigable and unsavory engine of pollution, the dog." (John Sparrow)

"The censure of a dog is something no man can stand." (Christopher Morley)

GANFYD

At the back of *This Book* and *That Book*, I asked readers to come up with ideas and suggestions. One reader who did was Dr. Peter Davies, a British physician, who sent me some examples of extraordinary requests for doctors' notes—under the heading Get a Note From Your Doctor (GANFYD)—collected from the Web site www.doctors.net.uk.

Letter requested . . .

To confirm that "I'm too breathless to cut the grass."

To confirm that a patient has an artificial limb.

To confirm that a patient's daughter is female, because the passport office had issued a passport with no stated sex on it.

To confirm that a sixteen-year-old girl does not have chicken pox.

To state that the doctor knows of no reason a student should not massage members of the public.

To give to a school so that the father isn't sent to jail for the child's nonattendance.

To say that "my daughter can appear in the school play."

To say that "my old-fashioned mobile phone is causing me tension headaches."

To say that "chewing gum at the checkout helps me breathe."

To confirm that a patient suffers backaches—so he can get a more comfortable BMW from his employer.

To confirm that a potential employee "is fit to handle cheese."

To confirm that a patient is fit to drive, even though she'd just received an eighteen-month driving ban.

To say that a patient's acne is so bad she cannot go to the gym (and so can get a refund).

To say that a patient's new coat caused a rash (so that the shop would give a refund).

It's Not Only the Patients

A vacation-insurance company asked whether a doctor would have said a patient was fit to travel had the doctor seen him before he left.

A school required a doctor's note before allowing a child with a leg in a plaster cast to be excused from swimming lessons.

One American state asks doctors to certify condemned prisoners as fit to be executed.

At a hospital: "That's a new problem, so before we can do anything you'll need to get a note from your general practitioner."

At a dentist's: "Due to pressure on the system, get a note from the doctor if you need to see the dentist."

A local bank phoned the doctor's office to ask for a note confirming that the customer "is who she says she is."

"Periodically it is necessary to obtain proof that pensioners are being paid correctly, and we would be grateful if you could complete this form to confirm that [X] is still alive."

Genuine Responses Given by Contestants on the British Version of *Family Feud*

Name something a blind person might use.
A sword.

Name an occupation where you need a torch.
A burglar.

Name a dangerous race.
The Arabs.

Name a bird with a long neck.
Naomi Campbell.

Name a number you have to memorize.
Seven.

Name something you might be allergic to.
Skiing.

Name a nonliving object with legs.
A plant.

Name something you do in the bathroom.
Decorate.

Name a domestic animal.
A leopard.

Name a part of the body beginning with n.
Knee.

Name something associated with the police.
Pigs.

Fish, Etc.

During low tides fiddler crabs darken in color and emerge from their burrows; during high tides they turn pale and retreat. Confined in a laboratory far away from the ocean, they still keep time with the tide, changing color as it ebbs and flows.

A killer whale torpedoes a shark from underneath, bursting the shark open through its stomach.

Dolphins don't breathe autonomically; breathing for them is a conscious act.

Jellyfish sometimes evaporate.

The Weddell seal can travel underwater for 7 miles without surfacing for air.

A male sea lion can go for 3 months without eating.

In the Caribbean there are oysters that can climb trees.

The lantern fish has a glowing spot on its head that would be bright enough to read by.

A starfish can move in any direction without having to turn, since it has no front or back.

Only one in a thousand creatures born in the sea reaches maturity.

Next to man, the porpoise is the most intelligent creature on Earth.

Shrimps and eels can swim backward as well as forward.

The flounder swims sideways.

A barnacle has the largest penis of any creature relative to its size.

The embryos of tiger sharks fight each other in the womb, and only survivors get born.

Octopuses have gardens (as Ringo knew).

An octopus's eye has a rectangular pupil.

Tuna swim at a steady rate of 9 miles per hour until they die—they never stop moving and would suffocate if they did. A tuna that lives fifteen years will have traveled a million miles in its lifetime.

The mudskipper is a fish that can walk on land.

The blue whale, the largest creature on earth, weighs approximately as much as 224,000 copies of *Moby-Dick*. Its heart beats 9 times a minute.

A lobster can lay 150,000 eggs at one time.

Texas horned toads can fire blood out of the corners of their eyes.

If you are served a crayfish with a straight tail, you shouldn't eat it. It was dead before it was cooked.

A baby gray whale drinks enough milk to fill more than 2,000 baby bottles a day.

Fish can taste with their tails and fins as well as their mouths.

Fish that live more than half a mile deep don't have eyes.

A sea urchin walks on its teeth.

Common eels die as they lay their eggs.

The bream hatches its eggs in its mouth.

The noise made by a pistol shrimp is so loud that it can shatter glass.

The koi carp can live for over two hundred years (although the average life span is about thirty years).

Crocodiles can't chew. They swallow and digest their food whole.

All shrimps are male at birth: some evolve to become female.

Fish cough.

Frogs have teeth, but toads don't.

Toads eat only prey that moves.

Dolphins can hear more than fourteen times better than humans can.

It can take the Galápagos turtle up to three weeks to digest a meal.

Sharks lay the largest eggs in the world.

Minnows have teeth in their throats.

Pairs of People Born on the Same Day

Joan Baez and Susannah York (January 9, 1941)

Federico Fellini and DeForest Kelley (January 20, 1920)

Carol Channing and Mario Lanza (January 31, 1921)

Lisa Marie Presley and Pauly Shore (February 1, 1968)

Fabian and Gayle Hunnicutt (February 6, 1943)

Joseph Mankiewicz and Max Baer (February 11, 1909)

Christina Ricci and Sarah Lancaster (Feburary 12, 1980)

Randy Crawford and Juice Newton (February 18, 1952)

Joe Bugner and William H. Macy (March 13, 1950)

Céline Dion and Donna D'Errico
(March 30, 1968)

Camille Paglia and Emmylou Harris (April 2, 1947)

David Letterman and Tom Clancy (April 12, 1947)

Benjamin Spock and Bing Crosby (May 2, 1903)

Olga Korbut and Debra Winger (May 16, 1955)

Malcolm X and Pol Pot (May 19, 1925)

Hergé and Laurence Olivier (May 22, 1907)

Lisa "Left Eye" Lopes and Paul Bettany (May 27, 1971)

Heidi Klum and Saffron Burrows (June 1, 1973)

Michael J. Fox and Aaron Sorkin (June 9, 1961)

Newt Gingrich and Barry Manilow (June 17, 1943)

John Goodman and Vikram Seth (June 20, 1952)

Jane Russell and Judy Holliday (June 21, 1921)

Todd Martin and Beck (July 8, 1970)

Marc Almond and Tom Hanks
(July 9, 1956)

Blake Edwards and Jason Robards
(July 26, 1922)

Alexander Fleming and
Louella Parsons
(August 6, 1881)

Gillian Anderson and Eric Bana (August 9, 1968)

David Copperfield and Mickey Rourke
(September 16, 1956)

Lance Armstrong and Jada Pinkett Smith (September 18, 1971)

Mika Hakkinen and Naomi Watts
(September 28, 1968)

John Entwistle and Peter Tosh (October 9, 1944)

Larry Mullen, Jr., and Peter Jackson
(October 31, 1961)

Shere Hite and Stefanie Powers (November 2, 1942)

Condoleeza Rice and Yanni (November 14, 1954)

Amy Grant and John F. Kennedy Jr. (November 25, 1960)

Jeff Bridges and Pamela Stephenson
(December 4, 1949)

Potatoes

Potatoes were first eaten more than six thousand years ago by natives (later Incas) living in the Andes mountains of Peru.

The Incas measured time by how long it took for potatoes to cook.

Their descendants, the Quechua Indians, have more than a thousand different names for potatoes.

Sir Walter Raleigh introduced potatoes to Europe in the late sixteenth century and grew them at his Irish estate near Cork.

Religious leaders denounced the potato because it wasn't mentioned in the Bible.

Potatoes are the world's fourth food staple—after wheat, corn and rice.

Every year enough potatoes are grown on Earth to cover a four-lane highway circling the world six times.

Potatoes are grown worldwide in over 125 countries (even in space—in 1995). China is the world's largest producer.

King Louis XVI of France wore potato blossoms in his button-hole, while Marie Antoinette wore them in her hair.

The potato is about 80 percent water and 20 percent solids and is related to both the tomato and tobacco.

Mr. Potato Head was the first toy to be advertised on American television.

Some superstitious people say you should carry a potato in your pocket to ease the pain of a toothache.

165

The botanical name for the common potato is *Solanum tuberosum*.

If you unscrew a lightbulb and the bulb breaks, cut a potato in half and push the potato in the socket and turn. It should remove the remainder of the bulb.

In 1778, Prussia and Austria fought the Potato War, in which each side tried to starve the other by consuming their potato crop.

 Until the late eighteenth century, the French believed that potatoes caused leprosy.

During the Alaskan Klondike gold rush of the 1890s, potatoes were so valued for their vitamin C content that miners traded gold for them.

Bodies

Patrick Swayze has broken his left knee five times.

Ashton Kutcher has two webbed toes on his left foot.

George Clooney has stated in several interviews that he's suffered from ulcers.

Ewan McGregor, Jessica Simpson, Elton John and Peter Jackson have all had their eyes corrected by laser surgery.

Joe Pesci, Christopher Walken, Kiefer Sutherland, Dan Aykroyd and Kate Bosworth each have eyes of two different colors.

People and What They Are Allergic To

Warren Beatty—oysters

Lindsay Lohan—blueberries

David Duchovny—metal (on his body)

Carol Channing—bleach

Rosie O'Donnell—cats and horses

Drew Barrymore—bee stings and perfume

David Cassidy—garlic

Lleyton Hewitt—grass, horses and cats

Kyle MacLachlan—wool

Ioan Gruffudd—cats

Belinda Carlisle—wheat

Rene Russo—sesame

Gillian Anderson—cat hair

Brad Pitt—dogs

Hay Fever Sufferers

Tyra Banks, Tiger Woods, Michelle Wie, John Major, Steffi Graf, Nigel Mansell, Sergio García, Jesper Parnevik

People Who Survived Tuberculosis

Nelson Mandela, Saffron Burrows, Stewart Granger, Engelbert Humperdinck, Richard Harris, Tom Jones, Archbishop Desmond Tutu

Gout Sufferers

Sam Torrance, Sam Mendes, Carl Wilson, Joseph Conrad, Julius Caesar, John Milton, Dr. Samuel Johnson

Teetotalers

Bruce Willis, Elizabeth Taylor, Michael York, Tracey Ullman, George W. Bush, Naomi Campbell, Anne Robinson, David Beckham

Insomniacs

Mia Farrow, Winston Churchill, Alexandre Dumas, Alexander Pope, Colin Farrell, Justin Timberlake, Richard Burton, Ernest Hemingway, Groucho Marx, Audie Murphy

Gallstone Sufferers

Aristotle Onassis, Larry Hagman, Benazir Bhutto, Pope John Paul II, Harold Macmillan, Yasser Arafat

People Who've Had a Heart Murmur

Tony Blair, Arnold Schwarzenegger, Bridget Fonda, Retief Goosen, Rachel Hunter, Evander Holyfield, Elizabeth Taylor

People Who've Suffered from Obsessive-Compulsive Disorder

Emily Lloyd, Michelle Pfeiffer, Billy Bob Thornton, Winona Ryder, David Beckham, Woody Allen, Harrison Ford, Charles Dickens, Leonardo DiCaprio, Rose McGowan

People Who Had Bad Adolescent Acne

Vanessa Redgrave, Derek Jacobi, Elvis Presley, Ricky Martin, Keira Knightley

People with Beauty Spots

Madonna, Robert De Niro, Cheryl Ladd, Roger Moore, Cindy Crawford, Lisa Stansfield, Sherilyn Fenn, Marilyn Monroe

People Who've Used Hypnosis

Lisa Kudrow (for stopping smoking)

Melanie Griffith (for stopping smoking)

Britney Spears (for stopping biting her nails)

Jennifer Aniston (for stopping smoking)

Pat Benatar (for relaxing her vocal cords)

Courteney Cox (for stopping smoking)

Tori Spelling (for her fear of flying)

Christy Turlington (for stopping smoking)

Salma Hayek (for fear of snakes)

Catherine Deneuve (for stopping smoking)

People Who Are Color-Blind

Paul Newman, Rod Stewart, Jack Nicklaus, George Michael

People Who've Suffered From Serious Depression

Billy Joel, Elton John, Axl Rose, Sheryl Crow, Kenneth Branagh, Bill Paxton, Marie Osmond

People Who Used to Mutilate Themselves

Johnny Depp used to cut himself (the small knife scars on his arms marked certain rites of passage).

Christina Ricci used to stub out burning cigarettes on her body and gouge herself with bottle tops. Interestingly, Ricci and Depp costarred in *Sleepy Hollow*.

Princess Diana used to cut herself with a penknife.

Shirley Manson, as a teenager, used to slash her legs with a razor.

People Who Wore Braces on Their Teeth as Adults

Jill St John, Jack Klugman, Diana Ross, Carol Burnett, Cher, Tom Cruise

People Who Say They Hate Their Feet

Britney Spears, Naomi Campbell, Claudia Schiffer, Kevin McNally

People Who Had Their Spleen Removed

Keanu Reeves, Bob Hawke, Burt Reynolds

People Who Had a Lung Removed

Tupac Shakur, Václav Havel, Link Wray, Stewart Granger, King George VI

Insects, Etc.

Anteaters would rather eat termites.

The world's smallest winged insect is the Tanzanian parasitic wasp, which is smaller than a housefly's eye.

A large swarm of locusts can eat 80,000 tons of corn in a day.

A spider dismantling its web is a sure sign of a storm on the way.

It is said that 80 percent of the creatures on Earth have six legs.

The cockroach is the fastest thing on six legs: it can cover a meter a second.

Bloodsucking hookworms inhabit 700 million people worldwide.

Crickets "hear" through their knees.

Snails breathe through their feet.

Maggots were once used to treat a bone infection called osteomyelitis.

There are 1 million ants for every person in the world.

The Madagascan hissing cockroach gives birth to live young (rather than laying eggs)—it is one of very few insects to do this.

The Venus flytrap takes less than half a second to slam shut on an insect.

Tarantulas extend and withdraw their legs by controlling the amount of blood pumped into them.

If you put a drop of alcohol on a scorpion, it will go mad and sting itself to death.

Dragonflies can fly at 30 miles per hour.

A species of earthworm in Australia can grow to about 10 feet long.

Many hairy caterpillars carry a toxin that can be painful to humans if touched.

On waking, ants stretch and appear to yawn in a very human manner.

From hatching to pupation, a caterpillar increases its body size 30,000 times.

Only full-grown male crickets can chirp.

The largest insect on Earth is the South American acteon beetle (*Megasoma acteon*), which measures 3.5 inches by 2 inches and is 1.5 inches thick.

The largest insects that ever lived were giant dragonflies with wingspans of 36 inches.

The heaviest insect is the goliath beetle, weighing in at over 100 ounces.

The neck of the male long-necked weevil is twice as long as its body.

The color of a head louse can depend on the color of its human host's hair.

The sound made by bees, mosquitoes and other buzzing insects comes from their rapidly moving wings.

Monarch butterflies regularly migrate between southern Canada and central Mexico, a distance of 2,500 miles. They weigh less than .02 ounces, travel at 20 miles per hour and reach altitudes of 9,500 feet.

A scorpion could withstand 200 times more nuclear radiation than a human could.

Cockroaches like to eat the glue on the back of stamps.

The fastest Lepidoptera are the sphinx moths. They have been recorded at speeds of 37 miles per hour.

Mosquito repellents don't repel mosquitoes but rather prevent the mosquitoes from knowing you are there by blocking their sensors.

Termites will eat your house twice as fast if you play them loud music.

The silkworm, *Bombix mori,* is the only truly domesticated insect. The adult moths are so tame they can barely fly and must be fed by hand. About 10 pounds of mulberry leaves are needed for silkworms to manufacture 1 pound of cocoons, from which can be spun 100 miles of silk thread.

The rarest breed of millipede has approximately 750 legs: more common breeds have between 80 and 400 legs.

Amazon ants can do nothing but fight, so they steal the larvae of other ants and then keep them as slaves.

There are some 200 million insects for every person in the world.

An ant, when intoxicated, will always fall over to its right side.

Every year insects consume 10 percent of the world's food supply.

When the female spider dies, she is eaten by her babies.

Moths aren't attracted to light: they fly toward the darkest point, which is behind the light.

Snails can live for up to 10 years.

Avid Painters

Michelle Pfeiffer, Josh Hartnett, Heath Ledger, Marilyn Manson, Pierce Brosnan, Christopher Walken, Arnold Schwarzenegger, Donna Summer, Sean Connery, Prince Charles, David Bowie, Björk, Lauren Hill, Sting, Elton John, Peter Gabriel, Cliff Richard, Brian May, Debbie Harry, Bob Dylan, Bob Geldof, John Lithgow, Jane Seymour, Jeff Bridges, Viggo Mortensen, Dennis Hopper

Good at Home Improvement

Bill Wyman, Daniel Day-Lewis, Sandra Bullock, Tim Allen

Avid Poker Players

Tobey Maguire, Jennifer Aniston, James Woods, Leonardo DiCaprio, Stephen Fry, Ricky Gervais, Joan Collins, Guy Ritchie, Salman Rushdie, Zara Phillips

Railway Enthusiasts

Timothy West, Phil Collins, Michael Palin, Rod Stewart (collects miniature train sets), Patrick Stewart

Avid Scrabble Players

Eno, Ginger Baker, Laura Davies, Guy Ritchie, Chris Martin, Moby

Avid Photographers

Viggo Mortensen, Prince Harry, Prince Andrew, Karl Lagerfeld, Helena Christensen, Bryan Adams, Jeff Bridges, Mary-Kate Olsen

Avid Gardeners

Michael Caine, Elizabeth Hurley, Edward Fox, Sam Neill, Lynn Redgrave, Matthew Modine

Avid Bridge Players

Omar Sharif, Arnold Palmer, Damon Albarn, Martina Navratilova, Stephen Fry, Sting

Hobbies Include Sleeping

Terry Jones, Jon Bon Jovi

Avid Cyclists

Madonna, Brad Pitt, Eva Mendes,
Mena Suvari, Olivia Williams,
Robin Williams, Woody
Harrelson, George W. Bush

Bungee Jumpers

Orlando Bloom, Prince William, Robbie Williams

Around the World

In Italy the entire town of Capena, just north of Rome, lights up cigarettes each year at the Festival of St. Anthony. This tradition is centuries old, and even young children take part (though there are now moves to stop the smoking or at least revert to smoking rosemary, the traditional substance).

A difference of almost three inches in height separates the average North Korean seven-year-old from the average South Korean seven-year-old—the South Korean child is the taller.

It is the custom in Morocco for a bride to keep her eyes closed throughout the marriage ceremony.

The Aymara guides of Bolivia are said to be able to keep pace with a trotting horse for a distance of about 62 miles.

The province of Alberta in Canada has been completely free of rats since 1905.

The O' prefix in Irish surnames means "grandson of."

There are more Barbie dolls in Italy than Canadians in Canada.

There are more than 15,000 different varieties of rice.

In China the entire population of over a billion shares only about 200 family names.

The Philippine flag is displayed with its blue field at the top in times of peace and the red field at the top in times of war.

The largest employer in the world is the Indian railway system, which employs over a million people.

Where the stones are of equal size, a flawless emerald is worth more than a flawless diamond.

In the Hebrides what defines an island is the ability of the land to support at least one sheep.

At any one time, 0.7 percent of the world's population is estimated to be drunk.

Aircraft are not allowed to fly over the Taj Mahal.

 The harmonica is the world's most popular musical instrument to play.

It used to be against the law in Swiss cities to slam the car door.

About 5,000 languages are spoken on Earth.

After oil, coffee is the most traded commodity in the world.

More than a hundred cars can drive side by side on the Monumental Axis in Brazil, the world's widest road.

Panama hats come from Ecuador.

Soldiers from every country salute with their right hand.

Dutch and Israeli soldiers aren't required to salute officers.

Bulgarians eat more yogurt than any other nationality.

The Tibetan mountain people use yak's milk as a form of currency.

Churches in Malta show two different (wrong) times in order to confuse the devil.

Rome has more homeless cats per square mile than any other city in the world.

In Bhutan all citizens officially become a year older on New Year's Day.

In Denmark the state pays for the disabled to have sex with a prostitute once a month.

At just 120 feet long, the D River in Lincoln City, Oregon, is the shortest river in the world.

There's an annual Thieves' Fair in France, where people are encouraged to try to steal things.

Ninety percent of Canadians live within 100 miles of the U.S. border.

Eccentric Events from Around the World

Summer Redneck Games (Georgia—includes spitball bug zapping, hubcap hurling, watermelon-seed spitting, bobbing for pigs' feet and the mud pit bellyflop)

Goat Racing (Pennsylvania)

World Shovel Race Championships (New Mexico)

Polar Bear Jump-Off (Alaska)

World Screaming Championships (Poland)

World Mosquito Killing Championship (Finland)

Stilton Cheese Rolling Competition (Stilton, U.K.)

World Nettle Eating Championships (Marshwood, U.K.)

Air Guitar World Championships (Finland)

World Walking the Plank Championships (Isle of Sheppey, U.K.)

World Bog Snorkeling Championships (Llanwrtyd Wells, Wales)

World Gurning Championships (Egremont, U.K.)

The Munich Festival Beer Drinking Challenge (Germany)

Odalengo Truffle Hunting Competition (Italy)

World Pea Throwing Competition (Lewes, U.K.)

Kiruna Snowball Throwing Contest (Sweden)

Trie-sur-Baïse Pig Screaming Championship (France)

Biggest Liar in the World Competition
(Santon Bridge, U.K.)

The World Wife Carrying Championships (Finland)

Burning Tar Barrels (Ottery St. Mary, U.K.)

Australia Day Cockroach Races (Australia)

Tuna Throwing (Australia)

World Worm Charming Championships (Nantwich, U.K.)

Penny Farthing World Championships (Tasmania)

The Great Mushroom Hunt Championships (Illinois)

Annual Bat Flight Breakfast (New Mexico)

Bognor Birdman Competition (Bognor Regis, U.K.)

The Great Tomato Fight (Spain)

Annual Roadkill Cook-Off (West Virginia)

**World's Championship Duck Calling Contest and Wings Over the
Prairie Festival** (Arkansas)

Annual World Elephant Polo Association Championships
(Kathmandu, Nepal)

Scarecrow Festival (Wray, U.K.)

The World's Twenty-One Most-Visited Countries (in order)

France

Spain

China (including Hong Kong)

United States

Italy

China

United Kingdom

Austria

Mexico

Germany

Canada

Hungary

Greece

Poland

Turkey

Portugal

Malaysia

Thailand

Netherlands

Russia

Sweden

How the Time Taken to Circumnavigate the World Has Been Lowered (*denotes single-handed)

*2005—Ellen Macarthur: 71 days, 14 hours, 18 minutes and 33 seconds

> ***2004**—Francis Joyon: 72 days, 22 hours and 54 minutes

2004—Steve Fossett: 58 days

> **2002**—Bruno Peyron: 64 days

1997—Olivier de Kersauzon: 71 days

> **1994–95**—Robin Knox-Johnston/Peter Blake: 74 days

1993–94—Bruno Peyron: 79 days

> ***1989–90**—Titouan Lamazou: 109 days

*1985–86—Dodge Morgan: 150 days

> **1983–84**—John Ridgway: 193 days

*1970–71—Chay Blyth: 293 days

> ***1968–69** Robin Knox-Johnston: 313 days (This was the first nonstop solo circumnavigation, and it was achieved under the auspices of a competition called the Golden Globe. Knox-Johnston was the only

sailor—of the eleven who set out at the same time as he did—to make it around the world: the others all had to turn back or give up.)

*1966–67 Francis Chichester: 274 days—stopping in Sydney for 48 days. (This was the first one-stop solo circumnavigation. He was sixty-five years old but was no stranger to record breaking, having become, in 1931, the first person to fly solo across the Tasman Sea.)

Note also: In 1519, Ferdinand Magellan led a convoy of five ships around the world. This first circumnavigation was an attempt to prove that the coveted Spice Islands were actually the property of Spain. Finding a direct route between the Spice Islands and Spanish Peru would be argument enough for ownership of these lands. Ferdinand Magellan set out from Spain with five ships, but the voyage was more difficult than expected. Disease, bad weather and loss of ships to Portuguese attack hampered them. On April 27, 1521, Magellan was killed in the Philippine Islands attempting to convert a native chief to Christianity. With only two ships remaining, the crew continued

the voyage; just one ship made it back to Seville with only eighteen crew members. The first circumnavigation of the globe had been completed.

The first (stopping) single-handed circumnavigation of the world was achieved by the American Joshua Slocum in 1898. His voyage on *Spray* began on April 24, 1895, when he was fifty-one years old. Over three years later, he returned on June 27, 1898. There's a sad footnote to this endeavor: on Nov. 14, 1909, Captain Slocum sailed *Spray* out of Martha's Vineyard bound for South America and was never heard from again.

The first nonstop single-handed circumnavigation by a woman was achieved by Kay Cottee in 1987–88. It took her 189 days.

The youngest person to achieve a nonstop single-handed circumnavigation was Jesse Martin in 1999 at the age of eighteen. It took him 327 days.

Then there was Alec Rose, who in 1968 returned home to a hero's welcome after sailing around the world in 354 days (with stops). He was a fifty-nine-year-old Portsmouth greengrocer who had bought, equipped and fitted his thirty-six-foot ketch, *Lively Lady,* all by himself. There was no team behind him and no high-tech equipment. Sir Alec (as he became) was quoted as saying, "I said my prayers quite often on this trip." Unlike Dame Ellen, who is expected to earn some £5 million as the result of her achievement, Sir Alec returned to working in his shop.

The Wit of Oscar Wilde

"The only thing to do with good advice is pass it on. It is never any use to oneself."

"Experience is the name everyone gives to their mistakes."

"Illness of any kind is hardly a thing to be encouraged in others. Health is the primary duty of life."

"Fashion is a form of ugliness so intolerable that we have to alter it every six months."

"I am not young enough to know everything."

"I think that God in creating Man somewhat overestimated his ability."

"Seriousness is the only refuge of the shallow."

"It is better to have a permanent income than to be fascinating."

"Whenever people agree with me I always feel I must be wrong."

"A little sincerity is a dangerous thing, and a great deal of it is absolutely fatal."

"To disagree with three-fourths of the British public is one of the first requisites of sanity."

"**Only dull people** are brilliant at breakfast."

"**It is absurd** to divide people into good and bad. People are either charming or tedious."

"**One should always** play fairly when one has the winning cards."

"**Anybody can sympathize** with the sufferings of a friend, but it requires a very fine nature to sympathize with a friend's success."

"**We're all in** the gutter, but some of us are looking at the stars."

Geography

The surface of the Dead Sea is more than 400 yards below the surface of the Mediterranean Sea.

Every gallon of seawater holds more than 4 ounces of salt.

Finland has more islands than any other country: 179,584.

Five hundred million years ago, Antarctica was on the equator.

More than 75 percent of the countries in the world are north of the equator.

Two minor earthquakes occur every minute.

Sahara means "desert" in Arabic.

The largest iceberg ever recorded was larger than Belgium. It was 200 miles long and 60 miles wide.

Five countries in Europe touch only one other: Portugal, Denmark, San Marino, Vatican City and Monaco.

The U.S. national anthem doesn't mention the name of the country; neither does the Dutch one. (In fact, you have to find an ancient and no-longer-sung verse of "God Save the Queen" to find any mention of Britain.)

The Swiss flag is square.

Less than 2 percent of the water on Earth is fresh.

Canada derives its name from a Native American word meaning "big village."

The oldest exposed surface on Earth is New Zealand's South Island.

England is smaller than New England.

The Eiffel Tower has 2.5 million rivets, 1,792 steps and can vary in height (according to the temperature) by as much as 6 inches.

As a result of precipitation, for a few weeks every year K2 is taller than Everest.

If the Earth were smooth, the oceans would cover its entire surface area—197 million square miles—to a depth of 12,000 feet.

The forests on Kauai in Hawaii are fertilized by dust from the deserts of China, 9,660 miles away.

A sizable oak tree gives off 28,000 gallons of moisture during the growing season.

The African baobab tree is pollinated by bats, and its blossom opens only to moonlight.

The national anthem of the Netherlands, the "Wilhelmus," takes the form of an acrostic. The first letter of each of the fifteen verses represent the name Willem van Nassov, or William of Orange. It is also the oldest anthem in the world.

Olympus Mons on Mars is the largest volcano in our solar system.

In May 1948, Mount Ruapehu and Mount Ngauruhoe, both in New Zealand, erupted simultaneously.

The Indonesian island of Sumatra has the world's largest flower: the *Rafflesia arnoldi*, which can grow to the size of an umbrella.

South Africa produces two-thirds of the world's gold.

Angel Falls in Venezuela is nearly 20 times taller than Niagara Falls.

Today There Are About 6.581 Billion People on Our Planet . . .

Here are the best projections for the future:

2007: 6.676 billion

2008: 6.773 billion

2009: 6.872 billion

2010: 6.972 billion

2015: 7.494 billion

2020: 8.056 billion

2025: 8.660 billion

2030: 9.308 billion

2035: 10.006 billion

Words

The word AND can be used five times in a row in the following sentence about a sign being painted above a shop called Jones and Son: Mr. Jones looks at the sign and says to the painter, "I would like bigger gaps between 'Jones' and 'and,' and 'and' and 'Son.'"

The word HAD can be used eleven times in a row in the following sentence about two boys, John and Steve, who had written similar sentences in their essays: "John, where Steve had had 'had,' had had 'had had'; 'had had' had had the higher mark."

The words LOOSEN and UNLOOSEN mean the same thing.

HIPPOPOTOMONSTROSESQUIPEDALIOPHOBIA is the fear of long words.

The first letters of the months July to November spell the name JASON.

CERUMEN is the technical term for earwax.

The oldest word in the English language is TOWN.

The word COFFEE came from Arabic and meant excitement."

The word VOODOO comes from a West African word that means "spirit" or "deity" and has no negative connotations.

The phrase SLEEP TIGHT originated when ropes around a wooden frame were used to support a mattress. Sagging ropes could be tightened with a bed key.

CRACK gets its name from the crackling sound it makes when smoked.

ALMA MATER means "bountiful mother."

The youngest letters in the English language are J, V and W.

The word **DIASTEMA** describes a gap between the front teeth.

The names for the numbers "eleven" and "twelve" in English come from the Anglo-Saxon for "one left" (*aend-lefene*) and "two left" (*twa-lefene*). They represented going back to your left hand and starting again after reaching ten counting on your fingers.

The stars and colors you see when you rub your eyes are called PHOSPHENES.

No word in the English language rhymes with pint, diamond or purple.

The magic word ABRACADABRA was originally intended for the specific purpose of curing hay fever.

John Milton used 8,000 different words in *Paradise Lost*.

The word MONOSYLLABLE has five syllables.

Ten human body parts are only three letters long: EYE, HIP, ARM, LEG, EAR, TOE, JAW, RIB, LIP, GUM.

The word LETHOLOGICA describes the state of forgetting the word you want.

The suffix OLOGY means the study of something. The shortest OLOGY is OOLOGY—the study of eggs.

The word STARBOARD is derived from the Old English word for the paddle that Vikings used on the right side of their ships to steer: *steorbord*.

Jonathan Coe's *The Rotters' Club* contains a 13,955-word sentence—the longest sentence in literature.

People with initials that spell out GOD or ACE are likely to live longer than people whose initials spell out words like RAT or PIG.

French author Michel Thaler published a 233-page novel that has no verbs.

If you exclude acronyms like RSVP, SHH, GRR, PSST, ZZZ and NTH are some of the rare words with no vowels (and no Y).

ZZZ is the longest word that you can type in the lower row of letters on a QWERTY keyboard.

FICKLEHEADED and FIDDLEDEEDEE are the longest English words that use only the letters in the first half of the alphabet.

NONSUPPORTS is the longest English word that uses only the letters in the second half of the alphabet.

The longest English words composed solely of letters that each have 180-degree rotational symmetry are SOONISH and ONIONS.

IOU does not stand for "I owe you." It stands for "I owe unto."

SPOONFEED is the longest word with its letters in reverse alphabetical order.

COUSCOUS is the only eight-letter English word that looks the same in uppercase and lowercase.

RUGGED and AGUE are two-syllable words that can be turned into one-syllable words by the addition of two letters (SH to make SHRUGGED; PL to make PLAGUE).

ARE and CAME are one-syllable words that can be turned into three-syllable words by the addition of just one letter at the end (A to make AREA; O to make CAMEO).

People Who've Suffered From Dyslexia

Salma Hayek, Keira Knightley, Ozzy Osbourne, George Patton, Princess Beatrice

The Most Beautiful Words in the English Language?

In 2004, to mark its seventieth anniversary, the British Council polled seven thousand people in forty-six countries to ask them what they considered to be the most beautiful words in the English language. There was also an online poll that attracted over 35,000 votes. Here are the results:

1. mother

2. passion

3. smile

4. love

5. eternity

6. fantastic

7. destiny

8. freedom

9. liberty

10. tranquillity

11. peace

12. blossom

13. sunshine

14. sweetheart

15. gorgeous

16. cherish

17. enthusiasm

18. hope

19. grace

20. rainbow

21. blue

22. sunflower

23. twinkle

24. serendipity

25. bliss

26. lullaby

27. sophisticated

28. renaissance

29. cute

30. cozy

31. butterfly

32. galaxy

33. hilarious

34. moment

35. extravaganza

36. aqua

37. sentiment

38. cosmopolitan

39. bubble

40. pumpkin

41. banana

42. lollipop

43. if

44. bumblebee

45. giggle

46. paradox

47. delicacy

48. peekaboo

49. umbrella

50. kangaroo

51. flabbergasted

52. hippopotamus

53. gothic

54. coconut

55. smashing

56. whoops

57. tickle

58. loquacious

59. flip-flop

60. smithereens

61. oy

62. gazebo

63. hiccup

64. hodgepodge

65. shipshape

66. explosion

67. fuselage

68. zing

69. gum

70. hen night

Lost in Translation

According to a poll of a thousand translators, the most untranslatable word in the world is ILUNGA, from the Bantu language of Tshiluba, meaning a person ready to forgive an abuse the first time, tolerate it the second time, but neither the third time. The runners-up were:

SHLIMAZL, Yiddish for a chronically unlucky person

RADIOUKACZ, Polish for a person who worked as a telegrapher for the resistance movements on the Soviet side of the Iron Curtain

NAA, Japanese word used only in Kansai area of Japan for emphasis or to agree with someone

ALTAHMAM, Arabic for a kind of deep sadness

GEZELLIG, Dutch for cozy

SAUDADE, Portuguese for a certain type of longing

SELATHIRUPAVAR, Tamil for a certain type of truancy

POCHEMUCHKA, Russian for a person who asks a lot of questions

KLLOSHAR, Albanian for loser

Pangrams (phrase or sentence that uses every single letter of the alphabet)

The quick brown fox jumps over a lazy dog.

Xylophone wizard begets quick jive form.

Wet squid's inky haze veils sex of jumping crab.

Jackdaws love my big sphinx of quartz.

Pack my box with five dozen liquor jugs.

The five boxing wizards jump quickly.

Quick wafting zephyrs vex bold Jim.

Mr. Jock, TV quiz Ph.D., bags few lynx.

Six plump boys guzzling cheap raw vodka quite joyfully.

XV quick nymphs beg fjord waltz.

Palindromes (phrases that read the same forward and backward)

Some men interpret nine memos.

Star comedy by Democrats.

We panic in a pew.

Won't lovers revolt now?

Sex at noon taxes.

No, it is opposition.

Live not on evil.

Was it a car or a cat I saw?

Never odd or even.

Step on no pets.

Able was I ere I saw Elba.

Nurse, I spy Gypsies—run!

Pull up if I pull up.

Madam, I'm Adam.

A nut for a jar of tuna.

A Santa lived as a devil at NASA.

A Toyota.

Race fast, safe car.

A slut nixes sex in Tulsa.

Desserts, I stressed.

Doom an evil deed, liven a mood.

Not New York, Roy went on.

Rot can rob a born actor.

Sit on a potato pan, Otis.

People Who've Been "Inside"

James Brown (carrying a gun and assault in 1988—served 2 years; he had also served 3 years for theft when he was a teenager)

Ozzy Osbourne (burglary—2 months in 1966)

Glen Campbell (sentenced to 10 days for drunk driving in 2004)

Don King (manslaughter in 1966—served 3 years, 11 months)

Zsa Zsa Gabor (slapping a cop—3 days in 1989)

Kelsey Grammer (drugs—2 weeks in jail for not doing the community service imposed for his offense in 1988)

Sean Penn (assault and violation of a probation order for an earlier assault—32 days in 1987)

Chuck Berry (violating the Mann Act by taking a girl across state borders for "immoral purposes"—2 years in 1962)

Ryan O'Neal (brawling—served 51 days in 1960)

Stephen Fry (stealing credit cards—spent 3 months in a young offenders' institution in 1975)

Paul McCartney (drugs—9 days in Japan in 1980)

Evel Knievel (assault in 1977—6 months)

Christian Slater (attacking policemen under the influence of cocaine—3 months in 1997)

Robert Downey Jr. (drugs—sentenced to 6 months in 1997)

Nick Nolte (reckless driving—30 nights in jail while at college, though he was released during the day to practice football)

Stacy Keach (drugs—sentenced to 6 months in 1984)

Wilson Pickett (drunk driving and causing injury—served a year in 1992)

David Crosby (drugs and possession of an illegal weapon—sentenced in 1983 to 5 years but served about a year and a half)

Muhammad Ali (a week in jail in 1968 for driving without a license. He was sentenced to 5 years in 1967 for refusing to serve in the army, but he challenged the verdict, it was overturned and he didn't spend any time in jail for it.)

Tim Allen (served 28 months in 1978 for attempting to sell cocaine)

Mark Wahlberg (convicted at the age of sixteen for his part in a robbery in which two Vietnamese were beaten—he served 45 days in jail)

Barry White (at the age of sixteen, for stealing tires)

Jeffrey Archer (sentenced to 4 years in 2001 for perjury and perverting the course of justice)

Celebrities Who Shoplifted

Farrah Fawcett (was twice arrested for shoplifting in L.A. before she was famous and was fined $500—although she claimed that she was acting in revenge because the stores in question refused to take back defective goods)

Quentin Tarantino (as a teenager, stole an Elmore Leonard novel from a local store)

John Lennon (in Holland, for shoplifting the harmonica he used on "Love Me Do")

Jill Clayburgh (caught stealing at Bloomingdale's "as a wild teenager")

Hedy Lamarr

Béatrice Dalle (in 1992, she was given a six-month suspended sentence for shoplifting £3,000 worth of jewelry in Paris)

Rufus Sewell (stole records in Woolworth and, as a starving drama student, was caught stealing food)

Courtney Love (she stole a Kiss T-shirt from a department store and was sent to a juvenile detention center)

Winona Ryder (in 2002 she was sentenced to 480 hours of community service, 3 years' probation, $3,700 in fines and $6,355 in restitution for shoplifting charges)

Tom Jones (he and his friends would steal singles from record shops: "In those days all the records used to be on display and, as a gang, we would buy one and come out with six or seven")

People Jailed for Tax Evasion

Al Capone (11 years in 1931)

Sophia Loren (17 days in 1982)

Chuck Berry (4 months in 1979)

Leona Helmsley (hotelier; 4 years in 1990)

Allen Klein (former Beatles manager; 2 months in 1979)

Marvin Mitchelson (American divorce lawyer; 2 years, 6 months in 1993)

Sun Myung Moon (14 months in 1984)

Aldo Gucci (fashion boss; 1 year in 1986)

Peter Max (artist; 2 months in 1998)

People Who Were Arrested

Hugh Grant (for performing a "lewd act" with Divine Brown in 1995—he was fined and given 2 years' probation)

Brigitte Bardot (for castrating a donkey that was trying to mount her donkey—later she was not only discharged but was also awarded costs against the plaintiff)

Johnny Depp (for trashing a hotel suite in 1994—he agreed to pay for the damage)

Billy Preston (for drunk driving and cocaine possession—given a suspended jail sentence and probation in 1992)

Johnny Cash (for being drunk and disorderly many times in the early 1960s)

Jodie Foster (for possession of cocaine—given a year's probation in 1983)

Harry Connick Jr. (for having a gun in his luggage at New York's JFK Airport)

Brian de Palma (for stealing a motorcycle and for resisting arrest—he was given a suspended sentence in 1963)

Carlos Santana (for marijuana possession—community service in 1991)

Paul Reubens (aka Pee-Wee Herman; for indecent exposure in a movie theater—he was fined and ordered to do community service)

Sean P. Diddy Combs (for possession of a firearm after a shooting incident at a bar in 1999) and Jennifer Lopez (arrested in the same incident and held in jail for 16 hours before being released without charge)

Chrissie Hynde (for demonstrating for animal rights in 2000. She used a knife to tear into leather and suede clothes in a Gap shop window in New York)

Jason Priestley (for drunk driving)

Vanilla Ice (after being accused of attacking his wife during an altercation in a car in 2001; he spent a night in jail in Florida)

Jennifer Capriati (for possession of marijuana in 1994; she was arrested in a hotel room and spent 23 days in a rehabilitation clinic)

People Whose Fathers Have Been in Jail

Keanu Reeves (Samuel Reeves—drugs)

Heather Mills-McCartney (John Mills—fraud)

Woody Harrelson (Charles Harrelson—murder)

Steffi Graf (Peter Graf—tax evasion)

Tatum O'Neal (Ryan O'Neal—brawling)

Stella McCartney (Paul McCartney—drugs)

Brittany Murphy (Angelo Bertolotti—a convicted mobster. After three jail sentences, he's alleged to have said, "I got friends who make Tony Soprano look like an altar boy.")

People Who've Had Computer Viruses Named After Them

Osama bin Laden, Avril Lavigne, Michelangelo, Tonya Harding

People Who Had Weapons Named After Them

Mikhail Kalashnikov (the Kalashnikov rifle)

William Mills (the Mills bomb)

Wilhelm and Peter Mauser (the Mauser magazine rifle)

Jim Bowie (the bowie knife)

Samuel Colt (the Colt revolver)

William Congreve (the Congreve rocket)

Oliver Winchester (the Winchester rifle)

Vyacheslav Molotov (the Molotov cocktail)

Bertha Krupp (Big Bertha mortar)

Henry Shrapnel (the shrapnel shell)

The Bible

The word "and" appears in the Bible 46,277 times.

The longest name in the Old Testament is Mahershalalhashbaz.

The Book of Esther in the Bible is the only book that doesn't mention the name of God.

The chapters in the New Testament weren't there originally. When medieval monks translated the Bible from the Greek, they divided it into chapters.

Scholars believe that what we now read as "forty," in Aramaic meant "many." So that "forty days," for example, simply meant "many days."

There are more than 1,700 references to gems and precious stones in the Bible.

There's no mention of rats in the Bible.

There are seven suicides recorded in the Bible.

The Human Condition

Your feet are bigger in the afternoon than at any other time of day.

The average talker sprays 300 microscopic saliva droplets per minute, about 2.5 droplets per word.

A fetus acquires fingerprints at the age of three months.

The Neanderthal's brain was bigger than yours is.

A nail grows from base to tip in about six months.

Beards have the fastest-growing hair on the human body. If a man never trimmed his beard, it could grow to over 30 feet in his lifetime.

Every human being spent about half an hour as a single cell.

One human hair can support a weight of over 6 ½ pounds.

The average man's speed of sperm emission is 11 miles per hour.

Every square inch of the human body has an average of 32 million bacteria on it.

Six-year-olds laugh about 300 times a day. Adults laugh about 15 times a day.

The attachment of the skin to muscles is what causes dimples. That and the gene that creates those muscles.

Kidneys filter about 500 gallons of blood each day.

One in every 2,000 babies is born with a tooth.

The largest cell in a woman is the ovum. The smallest cell in a man is the sperm.

The most common blood type in the world is type O. The rarest is AB.

The tendency toward ingrown toenails is hereditary.

The most sensitive finger is the forefinger.

The digestive tract is more than 30 feet long.

The ashes of the average cremated person weigh 9 pounds.

Blood makes up about 8 percent of the body's weight.

Due to gravitational effects, you weigh slightly less when the moon is directly overhead.

Every year about 98 percent of the atoms in your body are replaced.

The entire length of all the eyelashes shed by one person in an average lifetime is about 100 feet.

Your skull is made up of 29 different bones.

Hair is made from the same substance as fingernails.

Each square inch of human skin contains 20 feet of blood vessels.

During a twenty-four-hour period, the average human breathes 23,040 times.

The sound you hear when you put a shell to your ear is not the sea but blood flowing through your head.

Jaw muscles can provide about 200 pounds of force for chewing.

The human brain has about 100 billion nerve cells. Nerve impulses travel to and from the brain as fast as 170 miles per hour.

A cough comes out of your mouth at about 60 miles per hour.

If you unfolded your brain, it would cover an ironing board. The more wrinkles your brain has, the more intelligent you are.

Alcohol does not kill brain cells but rather detaches them. Reattachment would require new nervous tissue, which cannot be produced after about the age of five.

Your skin weighs twice as much as your brain.

There are 450 hairs in an average eyebrow.

The human brain stops growing at about the age of eighteen.

Your foot is the same length as the distance between your wrist and your elbow.

The chemicals in a human body are estimated to have a combined worth of around $8.

Humans can distinguish between 3,000 and 10,000 different smells.

The tongue is the fastest-healing part of the body.

Eighty-five percent of people can curl their tongue into a U shape.

Redheaded men are the most likely to go bald.

Eyes are composed of more than 2 million working parts.

Babies can breathe and swallow simultaneously until they're six months old.

Men's brains are about 10 percent heavier than women's.

A newborn baby sees the world upside down.

Middle-aged women wearing the scent of grapefruit seem six years younger to men (it doesn't work the other way around).

The human body is better suited to two four-hour sleep cycles than to one eight-hour cycle.

Rubbing the groove between your lips and your nose in a circular fashion helps to get rid of cravings for candy.

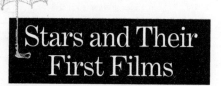

Stars and Their First Films

Julie Andrews—*Mary Poppins* (1964)

Dan Aykroyd—*1941* (1979)

Lauren Bacall—*To Have and Have Not* (1943)

Drew Barrymore—*Altered States* (1980)

Ned Beatty—*Deliverance* (1972)

Warren Beatty—*Splendor in the Grass* (1961)

Orlando Bloom—*Wilde* (1997)

      Helena Bonham Carter—*Lady Jane* (1984)

Marlon Brando—*The Men* (1950)

      James Caan—*Irma La Douce* (1963)

Nicolas Cage—*Fast Times at Ridgemont High* (1982)

      Sean Connery—*No Road Back* (1955)

Tom Cruise—*Endless Love* (1981)

      Willem Dafoe—*Heaven's Gate* (1980)

Robert De Niro—*The Wedding Party* (1963)

      Johnny Depp—*A Nightmare on Elm Street* (1984)

Danny DeVito—*Dreams of Glass* (1968)

      Clint Eastwood—*Revenge of the Creature* (1955)

Jane Fonda—*Tall Story* (1960)

      Richard Gere—*Report to the Commissioner* (1975)

Whoopi Goldberg—*The Color Purple* (1985)

      Jeff Goldblum—*Death Wish* (1974)

Hugh Grant—*Privileged* (1982, credited as "Hughie Grant")

      Melanie Griffith—*The Harrad Experiment* (1973)

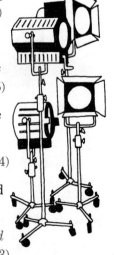

Gene Hackman—*Mad Dog Coll* (1961)

Goldie Hawn—*The One and Only Genuine Original Family Band* (1968)

Dustin Hoffman—*The Tiger Makes Out* (1967)

Anthony Hopkins—*The Lion in Winter* (1968)

Holly Hunter—*The Burning* (1981)

William Hurt—*Altered States* (1980)

Anjelica Huston—*Sinful Davey* (1968)

Jeremy Irons—*Nijinsky* (1980)

Scarlett Johansson—*North* (1994)

Michael Keaton—*Night Shift* (1982)

Kevin Kline—*Sophie's Choice* (1982)

Keira Knightley—*A Village Affair* (1994)

Lindsay Lohan—*The Parent Trap* (1998)

Jennifer Lopez—*My Little Girl* (1986)

Rob Lowe—*The Outsiders* (1983)

Shirley MacLaine—*The Trouble with Harry* (1955)

Tobey Maguire—*The Wizard* (1989)

Steve Martin—*Sgt. Pepper's Lonely Hearts Club Band* (1978)

Bette Midler—*Hawaii* (1965)

Sarah Miles—*Term of Trial* (1962)

Liza Minnelli—*Charlie Bubbles* (1968)

Eddie Murphy—*48 Hours* (1982)

Paul Newman—*The Silver Chalice* (1954)

Al Pacino—*Me, Natalie* (1969)

Sean Penn—*Taps* (1981)

Robert Redford—*War Hunt* (1961)

Keanu Reeves—*Youngblood* (1986)

Diana Rigg—*The Assassination Bureau* (1968)

Julia Roberts—*Blood Red* (1986)

Cybill Shepherd—*The Last Picture Show* (1971)

Sylvester Stallone—*A Party at Kitty and Stud's* (1970)

Terence Stamp—*Billy Budd* (1962)

Sharon Stone—*Stardust Memories* (1980)

Barbra Streisand—*Funny Girl* (1968)

Meryl Streep—*Julia* (1977)

Donald Sutherland—*The World Ten Times Over* (1963)

Lily Tomlin—*Nashville* (1975)

John Travolta—*The Devil's Rain* (1975)

Kathleen Turner—*Body Heat* (1981)

Jon Voight—*The Hour of the Gun* (1967)

Orson Welles—*Citizen Kane* (1941)

Robin Williams—*Popeye* (1980)

Bruce Willis—*Blind Date* (1987)

Actors and the Roles They Turned Down

Michael Douglas's role in *Romancing the Stone*—Sylvester Stallone

Jodie Foster's role in *The Silence of the Lambs*—Meg Ryan

Jack Lemmon's role in *Some Like It Hot*—Frank Sinatra

Uma Thurman's role in *The Avengers*—Gwyneth Paltrow

Patrick Swayze's role in *Ghost*—Bruce Willis

Al Pacino's role in *The Godfather*—Warren Beatty

Michael Douglas's role in *Traffic*—
Harrison Ford

> **Olivia Newton-John's** role in
> *Grease*—Susan Dey

Richard Gere's role in *Pretty Woman*—
Al Pacino

> **Harrison Ford's** role in *Star Wars*—Al Pacino

Christina Ricci's role in *The Ice Storm*—Natalie Portman

> **Mena Suvari's** role in *American Beauty*
> —Kirsten Dunst

> **Glenn Close's** role in *Fatal Attraction*—
> Miranda Richardson

> **Harrison Ford's** role in *Witness*—Paul Newman and
> Tom Selleck

> **Keanu Reeves's** role in *Speed*—Stephen Baldwin

> **Clint Eastwood's** role in *Dirty Harry*—Frank Sinatra

Peter O'Toole's role in *Lawrence of Arabia*—Albert
Finney

> **Cary Grant's** role in *Arsenic and Old Lace*—Bob Hope

Christopher Reeve's role in *Superman*—Robert Redford and
Steve McQueen

Actors Without a Single Oscar Among Them (apart from honorary Oscars)

Gene Kelly, Steve McQueen, Cary Grant, Glenn Ford, James Mason, Stewart Granger, Charles Boyer, Anthony Quayle, Montgomery Clift, Kirk Douglas, Greta Garbo, Agnes Moorehead, Carole Lombard, Barbara Stanwyck, Lana Turner, Judy Garland, Lee Remick, Natalie Wood, Rita Hayworth, Gloria Swanson

Actors Without Even a Single Oscar Nomination Among Them

Al Jolson, Tallulah Bankhead, Audie Murphy, Yvonne De Carlo, Errol Flynn, Hedy Lamarr, Dirk Bogarde, Raquel Welsh, Boris Karloff, Veronica Lake, Olivia Hussey, Glenn Ford, Jacqueline Bisset, Martin Sheen, Dorothy Lamour, Peter Cushing, Brigitte Bardot, Roger Moore, Jane Russell, Harry Belafonte

All the Years When English-Language Films Won the Palme d'Or at the Cannes Film Festival

2006—*The Wind That Shakes the Barley*

2004—*Fahrenheit 9/11*

2003—*Elephant*

2002—*The Pianist*

1996—*Secrets and Lies*

1994—*Pulp Fiction*

1993—*The Piano*

1991—*Barton Fink*

1990—*Wild at Heart*

1989—*Sex, Lies and Videotape*

1986—*The Mission*

1984—*Paris, Texas*

1982—*Missing*

1980—*All That Jazz*

1979—*Apocalypse Now*

1976—*Taxi Driver*

1974—*The Conversation*

1973—*Scarecrow* and *The Hireling*

1971—*The Go-Between*

1970—*M*A*S*H*

1969—*If . . .*

1967—*Blow-Up*

1965—*The Knack . . . and How to Get It*

1957—*Friendly Persuasion*

1955—*Marty*

1949—*The Third Man*

All the Years When English-Language Films Won the Golden Bear at the Berlin Film Festival (*denotes joint winner)

2003—*In This World*

2002—*Bloody Sunday**

2000—*Magnolia*

1999—*The Thin Red Line*

1997—*The People vs. Larry Flynt*

225

1996—*Sense and Sensibility*

1994—*In the Name of the Father*

1992—*Grand Canyon*

1990—*Music Box**

1989—*Rain Man*

1985—*Wetherby**

1984—*Love Streams*

1983—*Ascendancy**

1980—*Heartland**

1976—*Buffalo Bill and the Indians*

1974—*The Apprenticeship of Duddy Kravitz*

1966—*Cul-de-sac*

1962—*A Kind of Loving*

1957—*Twelve Angry Men*

1956—*Invitation to the Dance*

1954—*Hobson's Choice*

People Whose Names Appear in Film Titles

John Malkovich—*Being John Malkovich* (2000)

Greta Garbo—*Garbo Talks* (1984)

Brigitte Bardot—*Dear Brigitte* (1965)

Bela Lugosi—*Bela Lugosi Meets a Brooklyn Gorilla* (1952)

Douglas Fairbanks—*F as in Fairbanks* (1975)

Fred Astaire—*The Curse of Fred Astaire* (1984)

Ginger Rogers—*Ginger and Fred* (1986)

James Dean—*Come Back to the Five and Dime, Jimmy Dean, Jimmy Dean* (1982)

Humphrey Bogart—*The Man With Bogart's Face* (1980)

Clark Gable—*The Woman Who Married Clark Gable* (1985)

Errol Flynn—*In Like Flynn* (1985)

David Beckham—*Bend It Like Beckham* (2002)

Actors Who Won Nonacting Oscars

Matt Damon and Ben Affleck (Best Original Screenplay 1997: *Good Will Hunting*)

Clint Eastwood (Best Director 1992: *Unforgiven*; Best Director 2004, Best Film 2004)

Julian Fellowes (Best Original Screenplay 2001: *Gosford Park*)

Sofia Coppola (Best Original Screenplay 2003: *Lost in Translation*)

Robert Redford (Best Director 1980: *Ordinary People*)

Keith Carradine (Best Song 1975: "I'm Easy" from *Nashville*)

Emma Thompson (Best Adapted Screenplay 1995: *Sense and Sensibility*)

Kevin Costner (Best Director 1991: *Dances with Wolves*)

Michael Douglas (Best Picture 1975: *One Flew Over the Cuckoo's Nest*)

Mel Gibson (Best Director 1995: *Braveheart*)

Richard Attenborough (Best Director 1982: *Gandhi*)

Warren Beatty (Best Director 1981: *Reds*)

Uncredited Movie Appearances

Paula Abdul (in *Can't Buy Me Love*—as a cheerleader)

Steve Buscemi (in *Pulp Fiction*—as a waiter)

Cyd Charisse (in *Ziegfeld Follies*—as a dancer)

Don Cheadle (in *Rush Hour 2* and *Ocean's Eleven*—both times as a criminal)

Richard Dreyfuss (in *The Graduate*—as a student)

Kirsten Dunst (in *The Day After Tomorrow*—as a student)

Leif Garrett (in *Bob and Carol and Ted and Alice*—as the son of Dyan Cannon and Elliott Gould)

Charlton Heston (in the 2001 remake of *Planet of the Apes*—as Zaius, Thade's father)

Jason Isaacs (in *Resident Evil*—as Dr. Birkin)

Steve McQueen (in *Dixie Dynamite*—as a motorcyclist)

Christian Slater (in *Austin Powers: International Man of Mystery*—as a security guard)

Jaclyn Smith (in *Charlie's Angels: Full Throttle*—as Kelly Garrett, her character in the original TV series)

Actresses Who Shaved Their Heads for Roles

Sigourney Weaver (*Alien III*, 1992)

Emma Thompson (*Wit*, 2001)

Vanessa Redgrave (*Playing for Time*, 1980)

Demi Moore (*G.I. Jane*, 1997)

Alison Lohman (*Dragonfly*, 2002—though her scenes were cut)

Natalie Portman (*V for Vendetta*, 2005)

Persis Khambatta (*Star Trek: The Motion Picture*, 1979)

All the Winners of the American Film Institute's Lifetime Achievement Award

Sean Connery—2006

George Lucas—2005

Meryl Streep—2004

Robert De Niro—2003

Tom Hanks—2002

Barbra Streisand—2001

Harrison Ford—2000

Dustin Hoffman—1999

Robert Wise—1998

Martin Scorsese—1997

Clint Eastwood—1996

Steven Spielberg—1995

Jack Nicholson—1994

Elizabeth Taylor—1993

Sidney Poitier—1992

Kirk Douglas—1991

David Lean—1990

Gregory Peck—1989

Jack Lemmon—1988

Barbara Stanwyck—1987

Billy Wilder—1986

Gene Kelly—1985

Lillian Gish—1984

John Huston—1983

Frank Capra—1982

Fred Astaire—1981

James Stewart—1980

Alfred Hitchcock—1979

Henry Fonda—1978

Bette Davis—1977

William Wyler—1976

Orson Welles—1975

James Cagney—1974

John Ford—1973

Famous People Who Wrote/Cowrote Screenplays

Jack Nicholson (*Head*)

Martin Amis (*Saturn 3*)

Erich Segal (*Yellow Submarine*)

Roald Dahl (*You Only Live Twice*)

Paul Theroux (*Saint Jack*)

Clare Boothe Luce (*Come to the Stable*)

Actresses Who Tested for the Role of Scarlett O'Hara in *Gone With the Wind*

Lana Turner

Bette Davis

Norma Shearer

Miriam Hopkins

Tallulah Bankhead

Claudette Colbert

Katharine Hepburn

Loretta Young

Jean Harlow

Carole Lombard

People Who've Played God in Films or on TV

Morgan Freeman (*Bruce Almighty*, 2003)

James Garner (*God, the Devil and Bob*, 2000)

Alanis Morissette (*Dogma*, 1999)

Marianne Faithfull (*Absolutely Fabulous*, 1992)

Robert Morley (*Second Time Lucky*, 1984)

George Burns (*Oh, God!*, 1977)

Groucho Marx (*Skidoo*, 1968)

Martin Sheen (*Insight*, 1960)

Pop/Rock Groups That Appeared in Films

The Spice Girls—*Spice World* (1997)

Madness—*Take It or Leave It* (1981)

The Sex Pistols—*The Great Rock 'n' Roll Swindle* (1980)

The Who—*The Kids Are Alright* (1979)

Led Zeppelin—*The Song Remains the Same* (1976)

Slade—*Flame* (1975)

T-Rex—*Born to Boogie* (1972)

The Monkees—*Head* (1968)

Gerry and the Pacemakers—*Ferry Cross the Mersey* (1965)

The Beatles—*A Hard Day's Night* (1964), etc.

Bill Haley and His Comets—*Rock Around the Clock* (1956)

Things Said About Taxes

"Income tax returns are the most imaginative fiction being written today." (Herman Wouk)

"I have always paid income tax. I object only when it reaches a stage when I am threatened with having nothing left for my old age—which is due to start next Tuesday or Wednesday." (Noël Coward)

"There is no such thing as a good tax." (Winston Churchill)

"Next to being shot at and missed, nothing is really quite as satisfying as an income tax refund." (F. J. Raymond)

"In this world nothing can be said to be certain, except death and taxes." (Benjamin Franklin)

"There is no such thing as a good tax." (Winston Churchill)

"When they fire a rocket at Cape Canaveral, I feel as if I own it." (William Holden)

"There should be no taxation without comprehension." (John Gummer)

"The income tax has made more liars out of the American people than golf has." (Will Rogers)

"The avoidance of taxes is the only intellectual pursuit that carries any reward." (John Maynard Keynes)

"There's always somebody who is paid too much, and taxed too little—and it's always somebody else." (Cullen Hightower)

"The wages of sin are death, but by the time taxes are taken out, it's just sort of a tired feeling." (Paula Poundstone)

"Tax reform means 'Don't tax you, don't tax me, tax that fellow behind the tree.'" (Russell Long)

> **"Man is not** like other animals in the ways that are really significant: Animals have instincts, we have taxes." (Erving Goffman)

"Noah must have taken into the Ark two taxes, one male and one female. And did they multiply bountifully!" (Will Rogers)

The Longest-Serving British Monarchs Since 1066

Queen Victoria (64 years: 1837–1901)

     King George III (60 years: 1760–1820)

King Henry III (56 years: 1216–72)

     Queen Elizabeth II (54 years: 1952–)

King Edward III (50 years: 1327–77)

     Queen Elizabeth I (45 years: 1558–1603)

King Henry VI (39 years: 1422–61)

     King Henry VIII (38 years: 1509–47)

King Henry I (35 years: 1100–35)

     King Henry II (35 years: 1154–89)

King Edward I (35 years: 1272–1307)

Anagrams

LESS IN HARMONY—Shirley Manson

TRASH IN AIMING—Martina Hingis

BELT MERITED—Bette Midler

CAMEL NOISES—Monica Seles

VERY COOL TUNE—Courtney Love

BOIL JELLY—Billy Joel

INHALE? CHEERS!—Charlie Sheen

ARTICLES TARNISH—Christian Slater

LOW BORE—Rob Lowe

EMERGE ANGRIER—Germaine Greer

WE'LL SEND ANYONE—Lesley Anne Down

CREEP DID WARN—Prince Edward

EDIT WASN'T COOL—Clint Eastwood

AUTUMN HARM—Uma Thurman

BETRAY IN PRESS—Britney Spears

DARN SAD MALE—Adam Sandler

MERRY WARDROBE—Drew Barrymore

GERMANY—Meg Ryan

RAMPANT TOENAIL—Natalie Portman

LOWERS ULCERS—Russell Crowe

A ZIP SHALL RIP—Zara Phillips

SURE AM VAIN—Mena Suvari

I BULL, I SCREW—Bruce Willis

AN ACUTE GIRLISH AIR—Christina Aguilera

BUT MEN MOAN—Emma Bunton

HER MEN COLLAPSE—Elle MacPherson

VERY LESS TALL ON SET—Sylvester Stallone

SEMIBARKING—Kim Basinger

VOICE SELLS LOT—Elvis Costello

TALL, NOT DIM—Matt Dillon

SMOKES? TA!—Kate Moss

INTENSE HARM—Martin Sheen

TRY OLDER RAGE—Roger Daltrey

NO SNOB INANER—Anne Robinson

SMALL EASIER WIN—Serena Williams

AND A FILM ROLE—Alfred Molina

SHE'LL CHARGE MALE LIAR—Sarah Michelle Gellar

NIGHTLY INSTRUCTOR—Christy Turlington

I WIN SMALL BIRO—Robin Williams

OUR WAY IS REVENGE—Sigourney Weaver

PUT ON A RAVIOLI ACT—Luciano Pavarotti

DRY AND OKAY—Dan Aykroyd

O FAT MALE—Meat Loaf

UNSTABLE JERK? I'M IT!—Justin Timberlake

HAILED POSH—Sophie Dahl

WOW! LENGTHY PART—Gwyneth Paltrow

WORK? DIAL US!—Lisa Kudrow

I'M A KIND CLONE—Nicole Kidman

CASH IN NAME—Ian McShane

MAJOR LASS IN HEAT—Melissa Joan Hart

NOT INSANE ABROAD—Antonio Banderas

LET'S WIPE THE TEAPOT—Pete Postlethwaite

RAVAGE SAD NERVES—Vanessa Redgrave

RENT RISES? WHOOPEE!—Reese Witherspoon

ONE'S NOT RASH—Sharon Stone

REVENUE SAKE—Keanu Reeves

DOCILE FARTS—Fidel Castro

The Names of the Three Wise Monkeys

Mizaru (see no evil)

Mikazaru (hear no evil)

Mazaru (say no evil)

Dealing with Unsolicited Calls

Ask them if they're real or just one of the voices in your head.

> **Ask them** to spell their name. Then ask them to spell the name of their company. Then ask them where the company is located. Then ask them to spell the company's location.

Tell them to talk very V-E-R-Y S-L-O-W-L-Y, because you want to write down every single word.

> **If they** say they're not selling anything, tell them that that's a pity because you're in the mood for buying.

> **If they** give you their name—"Hi, I'm Sharon"—say, "Oh, Sharon, how *are* you?" as though they are a long-lost friend.

Tell them you're busy at the moment and could you have their home phone number to call them back later.

Adolf Hitler (with everything you already knew about him taken out)

As a child he was once beaten into a two-day coma by his father, Alois.

From 1925 to 1945, Hitler held the official title of SS Member #1. The man who was Member #2 wasn't Heinrich Himmler but Emil Maurice, Hitler's personal bodyguard/chauffeur and the man who is credited with founding the SS. Maurice, incredibly, was half Jewish, and when this came to light in 1935, he was thrown out of the SS. However, he was allowed to retain all his privileges.

Hitler's suicide in 1945 was not his first attempt. In 1923, after the failure of his putsch, he was hiding out in the attic of his follower Ernst "Putzi" Hanfstangl. When the police arrived, Hitler tried to shoot himself, but a policeman managed to stop him before he could pull the trigger.

Hitler was awarded the Iron Cross after being recommended for one by a Jewish officer.

He collected pornography and used to draw it.

He had an affair with his half sister's daughter, who eventually killed herself.

He was fascinated by hands and regularly consulted a book containing pictures and drawings of hands belonging to famous people throughout history.

Car manufacturer Henry Ford was the only American to get a favorable mention in Hitler's autobiography, *Mein Kampf*.

Hitler had Charlie Chaplin's *The Great Dictator* banned, but he was curious to see the film himself, so he had a print of the film smuggled into Germany from Portugal and watched it not once but twice.

Hitler esteemed Clark Gable above all other actors and during the war offered a sizable reward to anyone who could capture and bring Gable unscathed to him.

Four male descendants through his father's line were born between 1949 and 1965 in New York State. None of them had any children.

The U.S.A.

About a third of Americans flush the toilet while they are still sitting on it.

In Kentucky, 50 percent of people getting married for the first time are teenagers.

The dollar symbol ($) is said to be derived from a *U* combined with an *S*. Another theory is that it comes from the Spanish word *peso*.

Tennessee has more neighbors than any other state in the United States. It is bordered by eight states: Kentucky, Missouri, Arkansas, Mississippi, Alabama, Georgia, North Carolina and Virginia.

Many businesses in Nebraska have the word "Aksarben" in their names: such as Aksarben Five and Dime Store or Aksarben Transmission Service. Aksarben is Nebraska spelled backward.

During the time the atomic bomb was being hatched by the United States at Alamogordo, New Mexico, applicants for routine jobs were disqualified if they could read. Illiteracy was a job requirement. The reason: the authorities did not want their highly sensitive papers being read.

The name California was taken from a sixteenth-century Spanish novel, *The Exploits of Esplandian*, by Garci Ordóñez de Montalvo. In the novel it was the name of an imaginary island, described as an Amazon kingdom ruled by black women.

The three U.S. presidents who have faced real or impending impeachment—Andrew Johnson, Richard Nixon and Bill Clinton—also have in common that their names are euphemisms for the penis: johnson, dick and willie.

Every rise in the U.S. divorce rate is matched by a rise in toy sales.

There are more plastic flamingos in the United States than real ones.

Point Roberts in Washington State is cut off from the rest of the state by British Columbia, Canada. In order to get to Point Roberts from any other part of the state, you have to go through Canadian and U.S. customs.

The average American chews 190 pieces of gum each year.

In the 1940s the name of the Bich pen was changed to Bic out of concern that Americans would pronounce it "Bitch."

In Los Angeles there are more cars than people.

Deafness was once so common on Martha's Vineyard that all the people who lived there, both the hearing and the deaf, were fluent in their own dialect of sign language. No distinction was made in working or social life between those who could hear and those who could not. The gene for deafness was brought over in the seventeenth century by settlers from the Weald in Kent, and by the nineteenth century the rate of hereditary deafness on the island was 37 times the American average. Marriage to off-islanders eventually saw deafness disappear from the population; the last deaf islander died in 1952 (though deafness was still so unremarkable that her brief obituary in the *Vineyard Gazette* saw no reason to mention it).

Americans drink an average of 25 gallons of milk a year.

In Alaska it is an offense to push a living moose out of a moving airplane.

The New Yorker magazine has more subscribers in California than in New York.

In 1976 a Los Angeles secretary "married" her fifty-pound pet rock.

All the earthworms in America weigh 55 times what all the people weigh.

In 1980 a Las Vegas hospital suspended workers for running a pool on when patients would die.

Since January 1, 2004, the population of the United States has been increasing by one person every 12 seconds. Every 13 seconds someone dies, every 8 seconds someone is born, and every 25 seconds an immigrant arrives.

Seventy-two percent of Americans sign their pets' names on the greeting cards they send.

The United States consumes 25 percent of the world's energy.

On a clear day, you can see four states from the top of the Empire State Building: New York, New Jersey, Connecticut and Pennsylvania.

The largest living thing on earth (by volume) is the General Sherman Tree in Sequoia National Park. It is 275 feet tall, and its trunk is 37 feet in diameter at the widest point.

Second Street is the most common street name in the United States.

The U.S. government keeps its supply of silver at the military academy in West Point.

A party boat filled with sixty men and women capsized in Texas after it passed a nudist beach and all its passengers rushed to one side.

More than 8,100 U.S. troops are still listed as missing in action from the Korean War.

There's enough concrete in the Hoover Dam to make a 4-foot-wide belt around the equator.

The slogan on New Hampshire license plates is "Live Free or Die." The plates are made by inmates in the state prison.

In America there's a lawsuit filed every 30 seconds.

The average American walks 4 miles a year making the bed.

Every day 7 percent of the United States eats at McDonald's.

Americans eat more bananas than any other fruit.

The average American bank teller loses about $250 every year.

More Americans lose their virginity in June than in any other month because it's prom month and wedding month.

Every year Americans spend more than $5.4 billion on their pets.

The United States has 5 percent of the world's population but 25 percent of the world's prison population. It also has 70 percent of the world's lawyers.

Twenty percent of Americans think that the Sun orbits around the Earth.

More Americans were killed in the Civil War than in all other wars combined. However, more Americans have died in automobile accidents than in wars.

American tobacco auctioneers can speak up to 400 words per minute.

A typical American eats 28 pigs in a lifetime.

Goldfish swallowing started at Harvard in 1939.

Two in every 3 American car buyers pays the sticker price.

Thirty-two percent of all land in the United States is owned by the federal government.

For four years in the eighteenth century, there was a state called Franklin (named after Benjamin Franklin), but it was incorporated into Tennessee.

The average U.S. marriage lasts for just over 9 years.

Names

Kiefer Sutherland's full name is Kiefer William Frederick Dempsey George Rufus Sutherland.

People Known by Their Initials

W. H. (Wystan Hugh) Auden

J. G. (James Graham) Ballard

P. T. (Phineas Taylor) Barnum

J. M. (James Mathew) Barrie

H. E. (Herbert Ernest) Bates

J. J. (John Junior) Cale

G. K. (Gilbert Keith) Chesterton

J. M. (John Maxwell) Coetzee

e. e. (Edward Estlin) Cummings

F. W. (Frederik Willem) de Klerk

E. L. (Edgar Lawrence) Doctorow

T. S. (Thomas Stearns) Eliot

W. C. (William Claude) Fields

E. M. (Edward Morgan) Forster

W. S. (William Schwenck) Gilbert

D. W. (David Wark) Griffith

W. C. (William Christopher) Handy

L. P. (Leslie Poles) Hartley

A. E. (Alfred Edward) Housman

P. D. (Phyllis Dorothy) James

k. d. (Kathryn Dawn) lang

D. H. (David Herbert) Lawrence

T. E. (Thomas Edward) Lawrence

C. S. (Clive Staples) Lewis

A. A. (Alan Alexander) Milne

V. S. (Vidiadhar Surajprasad) Naipaul

P. J. (Patrick Jake) O'Rourke

J. C. (James Cash) Penney

J. D. (Jerome David) Salinger

O. J. (Orenthal James) Simpson

B. J. (Billy Joe) Thomas

J. R. R. (John Ronald Reuel) Tolkien

P. L. (Pamela Lyndon) Travers

J. M. W. (Joseph Mallord William) Turner

H. G. (Herbert George) Wells

P. G. (Pelham Grenville) Wodehouse

W. B. (William Butler) Yeats

Unusual Names Given by Celebrities to Their Children

Pilot Inspektor Riesgraf Lee—Jason Lee

Seven and Puma—Erykah Badu

Tu—Rob Morrow (i.e., Tu Morrow)

Salvador—Ed O'Brien

Deacon—Reese Witherspoon

Moses and Apple—Gwyneth Paltrow and Chris Martin

MaKena' Lei—Helen Hunt (after a Hawaiian island)

Salome—Alex Kingston

Camera—Arthur Ashe

Jack Daniel—Ellen Barkin and Gabriel Byrne

J.C.—Jackie Chan

Erika, Erinn, Ensa, Evin and Ennis—Bill Cosby

Lolita and Piper—Brian De Palma

Brandi and Buck—Roseanne

Cruz—David and Victoria Beckham

Ross and Chudney—Diana Ross

Gib and Prima—Connie Sellecca, Gil Gerard, and John Tesh

Jesse Mojo—Sam Shepard and O-Lan Jones

China—Grace Slick and Paul Kantner

Kal-el (Superman's real name)—Nicolas Cage

Paris and Brielle—Blair Underwood

Rio—Sean Young

Lourdes—Madonna

Cuathemoc—Louis Malle

Imani—Jasmine Guy

Emerson Rose—Teri Hatcher

Roan and Laird—Sharon Stone

Clementine—Claudia Schiffer

Atherton—Don Johnson

Paris, Prince Michael I and Prince II—Michael Jackson

Paris—Pierce Brosnan

Eja (boy)—Shania Twain

Tony Curtis, John Huston, John Leguizamo, Lord Byron and Donatella Versace all named a daughter Allegra.

People Who Found Fame with Just a First Name

Beck (Hansen)

Prince (Rogers Nelson)

Madonna (Ciccone)

Dion (Dimucci)

Sade (Adu)

Ann-Margret (Olsson)

Cher (Sarkisian)

Yanni (Chrysomallis)

RuPaul (Charles)

Donovan (Leitch)

Björk (Gudmundsdottir)

Seal (Seal is short for Sealhenry, and his surname is Samuel)

Taki (Theodoracopulos)

Arletty (Arletty was short for Arlette-Léonie, and her surname was Bathiat)

Des'ree (Des'ree is a variation on Desiree, and her surname is Weekes)

Fabian (Fabian is short for Fabiano, and his surname is Forte)

Tiffany (Darwisch)

Wynonna (Judd)

Dido (Dido Florian Cloud de Bounevialle Armstrong)

Aaliyah (Dana Haughton)

Brandy (Norwood)

Iman (Abdulmajid)

Jewel (Kilcher)

Kelis (Rogers)

Vendela (Thomessen)

People Who Found Fame with Just a Surname

(Annunzio Paolo) Mantovani

(Stephen) Morrissey

(Chaim) Topol

(Harry) Nilsson

(Wladziu Valentino) Liberace

(Michael) D'Angelo

(Josip Broz) Tito

People Who Found Fame with Just a Nickname/Sobriquet

Bono (Paul Hewson)

Capucine (Germaine Lefebvre)

Sting (Gordon Sumner)

Pelé (Edson Arantes do Nascimento)

Enya (Eithne Ní Bhraonáin)

Martika (Marta Marrero)

Fish (Derek Dick)

2Pac (Tupac Shakur)

Fernandel (Fernand Contandin)

Falco (Johann Holzel)

Vangelis (Evangelos Papathanassiou)

Coolio (Artis Ivey Jr.)

Divine (Harris Glen Milstead)

Eminem (Marshall Mathers)

Flea (Michael Balzary)

Hergé (Georges Remi)

Saki (Hector Munro)

Molière (Jean-Baptiste Poquelin)

Voltaire (François Marie Arouet)

Kool (Robert Bell)

Lemmy (Ian Fraser Kilminster)

Moby (Richard Hall)

Nena (Gabriele Kerner)

Nico (Christa Paffgen)

Pink (Alecia Moore)

Men with Women's Names

Dana Andrews

Val Kilmer

Marilyn Manson

Shirley Crabtree (original name of the wrestler Big Daddy)

Mandy Patinkin

Kay Kyser

Marion Morrison (original name of the actor John Wayne)

Lilian Thuram (French soccer player)

Women with Men's Names

Sean Young

Michael Learned

George Eliot

Cameron Diaz

Glenn Close

Jerry Hall

Daryl Hannah

George Sand

People Who Named Their Children After Other Famous People

Neneh Cherry: named daughter Tyson, after Mike Tyson

Dave Stewart and Siobhan Fahey: named son Django, after Django Reinhardt

Woody Allen: named his son Satchel, after Satchel Paige, the baseball player

Demi Moore and Bruce Willis: named one daughter Rumer, after the author Rumer Godden, and another daughter Tallulah, after Tallulah Bankhead

Ricky Schroder: named son Holden, after William Holden

Bryan Ferry: named son Otis, after Otis Redding

People Who Were Named After Someone/Something Famous

Penelope Cruz (after the song "Penélope" by Joan Manuel Serrat)

Sadie Frost (after the song "Sexy Sadie" by the Beatles)

Céline Dion (after the song "Céline" by Hugues Aufray)

Jude Law (after the song "Hey Jude" by the Beatles)

People Who Chose to Use Their Middle Name as a First Name

Christopher Ashton Kutcher

George Roger Waters

Patrick Ryan O'Neal

Lee Alexander McQueen

Robert Oliver Reed

John Anthony Quayle

James Harold Wilson

Marie Dionne Warwick

Ernestine Jane Russell

Ruth Bette Davis

Alfred Alistair Cooke

Norvell Oliver Hardy

Robert Edward, (i.e. Ted) Turner

Eldred Gregory Peck

Mary Sean Young

Daniel Patrick Macnee

David Paul Scofield

James Paul McCartney

Mary Farrah Fawcett

William Clark Gable

Ernest Ingmar Bergman

George Richard Chamberlain

Terrence Stephen (Steve) McQueen

Arthur John Gielgud

George Orson Welles

Howard Andrew (Andy) Williams

Troyal Garth Brooks

John Michael Crichton

Audrey Faith Hill

Nelust Wyclef Jean

Carole Penny Marshall

Margaret Jane Pauley

Isaac Donald Everly

Ellen Tyne Daly

Holly Michelle Phillips

Winnifred Jacqueline Bisset

Henry Ken(neth) Russell

Nicknames

Natalie Imbruglia—Jagger Lips and Frog Eyes

Benjamin Bratt—Scarecrow (because he was so thin)

Macy Gray—Bum Jiggy

Lucy Liu—Curious George (her friends' nickname for her)

J. C. Chasez—Mr. Sleepy

Madonna—Nonni (family nickname)

Johnny Depp—Mr. Stench

Kathy Bates—Bobo

Helen Mirren—Popper

People With Unusual Middle Names

Robbie MAXIMILIAN Williams

Richard TIFFANY Gere

Noah STRAUSSER SPEER Wyle

Courteney BASS Cox

Hugh MARSTON Hefner

Bob XENON Geldof

Famous Siblings With Different Surnames

Joan Fontaine and Olivia de Havilland

A. S. Byatt and Margaret Drabble

Emilio Estevez and Charlie Sheen

Warren Beatty and Shirley MacLaine

George Sanders and Tom Conway

Talia Shire and Francis Ford Coppola

Peter Graves and James Arness

Gypsy Rose Lee and June Havoc

Ashley Judd and Wynonna

Genuine Names for Lipsticks

Amour, Firecracker, Censored, Strawberry Fair, Corsaire, Nutmeg, Moon Beam, Neon Nude, Cool Candy, Passionate Pink, Mad Mauve, Risky Ruby, Portobello Plum, True Terracotta, Hot Honey, Barely Blush, Crazy Caramel, Too Truffle, Rolling Stone, Warm Platinum, Golden Spice, Chocoholic, Whisper, Fig, Parma Argent, Buttermilk, Sherbet Twist, Wine & Dine, Just Peachy, Hearts a Fire, So Cinnamon, In the Nude, Summer Daze, Let's Go Crazy

Countries That Changed Their Names

Rhodesia (to Zimbabwe)

Upper Volta (to Burkina Faso)

Aden (to Yemen)

Abyssinia (to Ethiopia)

Belgian Congo (to Zaire and back to Congo)

Dahomey (to Benin)

Siam (to Thailand)

Persia (to Iran)

Basutoland (to Lesotho)

British Honduras (to Belize)

Gold Coast (to Ghana)

Dutch Guiana (to Suriname)

Nyasaland (to Malawi)

The Afars and the Issas (to Djibouti)

Portuguese Guinea (to Guinea-Bissau)

Dutch East Indies (to Indonesia)

New Hebrides (to Vanuatu)

Bechuanaland (to Botswana)

Fictitious Places

Nutwood (*Rupert Bear*)

Llareggub (*Under Milk Wood*)

Gotham City (*Batman*)

St. Mary Mead (*The Murder at the Vicarage* and all the Agatha Christie films and novels featuring Jane Marple)

Witches

In 2000, students at St. Andrew's University tried to recruit 400 witches for a pagan coven.

Some years ago Italian soccer was hit by a witchcraft scandal when it was revealed that the manager of the first-division club, Pescara, had consulted a witch named Miriam Lebel. Apparently this was just the tip of the iceberg and witchcraft is rife in the Italian game.

In New York, witches organized themselves into an "Anti-Discrimination Lobby" in order to fight discrimination and to get a paid day off on Halloween.

In Gloucester, U.K. in 1992, a new minister demanded that his church be exorcised after he discovered that the organist, Shaun Pickering-Merrett, had been a practicing witch for six years.

In 2001, villagers in southern India set fire to four women and a man they accused of witchcraft. The five were burned alive.

Now that weddings can be held outside of churches and register offices, in 1996 a witches' coven in Worcestershire, U.K. put in an application for a license to carry out legal wedding services (or "handfasts").

Lois Bourne is a "white" (i.e., a good) witch from St. Albans, U.K. When friends complained that they hadn't been able to sell their house for four years, she cast a spell, and the next day the house received an offer. Mrs. Bourne modestly admitted that it could be a coincidence but anyway later said, "Selling houses is very boring magic, and I refuse to do it."

In 1995, Susan Leybourne, twenty-nine, a witch who had been ordained a pagan priestess at the Circle University in Louisiana, became the first witch to be named a chaplain at a British university after her (unpaid) appointment was requested by forty members of Leeds University's Occult Society.

In 1978 the British writer Nesta Wynn Ellis visited a witch doctor in Zimbabwe, who told her that in six months she would marry a man she hadn't yet met. She then went to another witch doctor, who told her the same. A month later, in Kenya, she met her future husband. Five months after that, they were married.

Iolanda Quinn, ex-wife of film star Anthony Quinn, is a self-confessed witch. When Quinn fathered a "love child," Mrs. Quinn said, "This baby is not his. You must believe me, I am a witch, and I know." Unfortunately for her, Quinn admitted being the father.

In Russia in 1995, Lyuba Lagutina, a publisher, went to a witch when her baby cried so much that he developed a hernia. The witch said a few spells, and the baby was miraculously cured.

In South Africa two so-called witches were recently burned to death after a bus crash killed fourteen children. Speelman Matsipane and Mamiagabo Makwele were accused of being witches on account of their advanced age. They were dragged from their homes and murdered. This is not the only case where witches (or women who are accused of being witches) have been blamed for accidents that had nothing to do with them. Whenever someone is struck by lightning in parts of South Africa, it is said to be the work of witches, and old ladies suspected of being witches are driven out of their homes.

Wise Words from Albert Einstein

"Only two things are infinite, the universe and human stupidity, and I'm not sure about the former."

"I never think of the future. It comes soon enough."

"The hardest thing in the world to understand is income tax."

"An empty stomach is not a good political adviser."

"Nationalism is an infantile disease. It is the measles of mankind."

"I can't believe that God plays dice with the universe."

Would Have Turned 100 in 2007

Rumer Godden, American writer

Peggy Ashcroft, British actress

Cab Calloway, American musician

Count Klaus von Stauffenberg, German anti-Hitler activist

Gene Autry, American actor and singer

Allan Jones, American actor and singer

Warren Burger, American Supreme Court chief justice

Louis MacNeice, British poet

Fay Wray, Canadian actress

Bernard Miles, British actor

Barbara Stanwyck, American actress

Feliks Topolski, British artist

George Romney, American politician

Jack Albertson, American actor

Rosalind Russell, American actress

T. E. B. Clarke, British screenwriter

Hergé, Belgian writer

Laurence Olivier, British actor

Katharine Hepburn, American actress

Fred Zinnemann, Austrian-born film director

Kate Smith, American singer

Leslie Charteris, British writer

Daphne du Maurier, British writer

John Wayne, American actor

Frank Whittle, British inventor

François "Papa Doc" Duvalier, Haitian dictator

Irving "Swifty" Lazar, American agent

Iron Eyes Cody, American actor

Jessie Matthews, British singer and actress

Buster Crabbe, American actor

W. H. Auden, British poet

Robert Young, American actor

Cesar Romero, American actor

Dan Duryea, American actor

Henry Cotton, British golfer

Ray Milland, American actor

Pierre Mendes-France, French politician

Alexander Knox, Canadian actor

James Michener, American author

Turn 90 in 2007

Ernest Borgnine, American actor

Michael Gough, British actor

Jo Stafford, American singer

Robert Byrd, American politician

Conor Cruise O'Brien, Irish writer

Arthur C. Clarke, British writer

Joan Fontaine, American actress

June Allyson, American actress

Herbert Lom, Czech-born actor

Caspar Weinberger, American politician

Lena Horne, American singer

Mel Ferrer, American actor

Sidney Sheldon, American writer

Zsa Zsa Gabor, American actress

Phyllis Diller, American comedienne

Would Have Turned 90 in 2007

Indira Gandhi, Indian politician

Heinrich Böll, German author

Tiny Rowland, British industrialist

Bobby Locke, South African golfer

Dizzy Gillespie, American musician

Thelonious Monk, American musician

Fernando Rey, French actor

Buddy Rich, American musician

Ferdinand Marcos, Philippine politician

Jessica Mitford, British writer

John Lee Hooker, American musician

Robert Mitchum, American actor

Richard Boone, American actor

Raymond Burr, Canadian actor

John F. Kennedy, American president

Dean Martin, American singer and actor

David Tomlinson, British actor

James Donald, British actor

Valerie Hobson, British actress

Rufus Thomas, American singer

Cyrus Vance, American politician

Robert Lowell, American poet

Desi Arnaz, American actor

Frankie Howerd, British comedian

Anthony Burgess, British writer

John Connally, American politician

Turn 80 in 2007

Roger Moore, British actor

Cleo Laine, British singer

Andy Williams, American singer

Honor Blackman, British actress

Ruth Prawer Jhabvala, German-born writer

Elisabeth Söderström, Swedish singer

Christopher Plummer, Canadian actor

Fidel Castro, Cuban leader

Estelle Parsons, American actress

Marcel Ophuls, French film director

Lee Grant, American actress

Frank Sedgman, Australian tennis player

Günter Grass, German writer

Al Martino, American singer

Tom Bosley, American actor

Freddie Jones, British actor

Robert Guillaume, American actor

Norm Crosby, American comedian

Rosemary Harris, British actress

Peter Falk, American actor

Gordon Scott, American actor

Rosalynn Carter, American First Lady

David Dinkins, American politician

Ken Russell, British film director

Eva Bartok, Hungarian-born actress

Gina Lollobrigida, Italian actress

Neil Simon, American playwright

Clint Walker, American actor

Edie Adams, American singer and actress

Mstislav Rostropovich, Russian musician

Mort Sahl, American writer and comedian

Sidney Poitier, American actor

Hubert de Givenchy, French fashion designer

Harry Belafonte, American singer

Juliette Greco, French singer

Eartha Kitt, American singer

John Kander, American composer

Lois Maxwell, Canadian actress

Harvey Korman, American actor

John Warner, American politician

Would Have Turned 80 in 2007

Coretta Scott King, American widow of Martin Luther King

Denis Quilley, British actor

Alan King, American comedian

George C. Scott, American actor

Gilbert Becaud, French singer/songwriter

Rachel Roberts, British actress

Althea Gibson, American tennis player

Robert Shaw, British actor

Janet Leigh, American actress

Bob Fosse, American choreographer and director

Brock Peters, American actor

Robert Ludlum, American writer

Herbert Ross, American film director

Daniel Patrick Moynihan, American politician

George Plimpton, American writer

Jack Cassidy, American actor

James Broderick, American actor

Stanley Baker, British actor

Johnnie Ray, American singer

Olof Palme, Swedish politician

Stan Getz, American musician

Turn 70 in 2007

James MacArthur, American actor

Jane Fonda, American actress

Anthony Hopkins, British actor

Yaphet Kotto, American actor

Ingrid Pitt, Polish-born actress

Frank Ifield, Australian singer

Ridley Scott, British film director

Loretta Swit, American actress

Tom Paxton, American singer/songwriter

Alan Ladd Jr., American film executive

Emile Ford, American singer

Merle Park, British ballerina

Brian Blessed, British actor

Virna Lisi, Italian actress

Tommy Sands, American singer

John Philip Law, American actor

Dustin Hoffman, American actor

Anna Massey, British actress

Robert Redford, American actor

Garth Hudson, Canadian musician

Steven Berkoff, British actor and writer

Bill Cosby, American actor

George Hamilton IV, American singer/songwriter

Tom Stoppard, British playwright

Vladimir Ashkenazy, Russian musician

Ned Beatty, American actor

Gene Chandler, American singer/songwriter

David Hockney, British artist

Erich Segal, American writer

Morgan Freeman, American actor

Colleen McCullough, Australian writer

Madeleine K. Albright, American politician

Trini Lopez, American singer and actor

Saddam Hussein, Iraqi dictator

Frankie Valli, American singer

Jack Nicholson, American actor

Colin Powell, American soldier and politician

Merle Haggard, American singer

Billy Dee Williams, American actor

Edward Fox, British actor

Warren Beatty, American actor

Valentina Tereshkova, Russian astronaut

Ivan Boesky, American businessman

Gary Lockwood, American actor

Seymour Hersh, American journalist

Tom Courtenay, British actor

Suzanne Pleshette, American actress

Don Everly, American singer

Tommy Smothers, American comedian

Stuart Damon, American actor

Vanessa Redgrave, British actress

Boris Spassky, Russian chess player

Margaret O'Brien, American actress

Dorothy Provine, American actress

Joseph Wambaugh, American writer

Grace Bumbry, American opera singer

Judith Krantz, American writer

Dyan Cannon, American actress

Would Have Turned 70 in 2007

Kerry Packer, Australian businessman

Sandy Dennis, American actress

Billy Carter, brother of American president Jimmy Carter

Waylon Jennings, American singer

Hunter S. Thompson, American writer

Graham Bond, British musician

Lorenzo Music, American TV producer

Allan Carr, American film producer

O'Kelly Isley, American singer

Peter Cook, British comedian

Turn 60 in 2007

Ben Cross, British actor

Susan Lucci, American actress

Ted Danson, American actor

Jeff Lynne, British musician

Dwight Schultz, American actor

Joe Walsh, American musician

277

David Mamet, American playwright

Jim Messina, American musician

Gregg Allman, American musician

Joe Mantegna, American actor

Richard Dreyfuss, American actor

Peter Noone, British singer

Hillary Rodham Clinton, American politician

Lee Meredith, American actress

Kevin Kline, American actor

Jaclyn Smith, American actress

Stephen Collins, American actor

Bob Weir, American guitarist

Sammy Hagar, American singer

David Zucker, American film director

Lol Creme, British musician/producer

Sam Neill, New Zealander actor

Stephen King, American writer

Cheryl Tiegs, American model

Lynn Anderson, American singer

Denis Lawson, British actor

Meat Loaf, American singer/songwriter

Julie Covington, British actress

Anne Archer, American actress

Cindy Williams, American actress

Barbara Bach, American actress

Ian Anderson, British musician

Danielle Steel, American writer

Carlos Santana, Mexican musician

Albert Brooks, American actor and director

Don Henley, American musician

Robert Hays, American actor

Arnold Schwarzenegger, Austrian-born actor and politician

Richard Griffiths, British actor

Bernie Leadon, American musician

Brian May, British musician

Betty Buckley, American actress

Arlo Guthrie, American singer/songwriter

Mitch Mitchell, British musician

O. J. Simpson, American football player and actor

Camilla Parker-Bowles, Duchess of Cornwall

Candy Clark, American actress

Meredith Baxter, American actress

Bryan Brown, Australian actor

Peter Weller, American actor

Laurie Anderson, American singer

Demis Roussos, Greek singer

Linda Thorson, British actress

Salman Rushdie, British writer

Sondra Locke, American actress

Jonathan Pryce, British actor

Ronnie Wood, British musician

Jo Ann Pflug, American actress

Warren Clarke, British actor

Ann Peebles, American singer

Tommy James, American singer

Johnny Miller, American golfer

Camille Paglia, American feminist

Emmylou Harris, American singer/songwriter

John Ratzenberger, American actor

Steve Howe, British musician

Bunny Wailer, Jamaican musician

David Letterman, American TV host

Tom Clancy, American writer

        Lois Chiles, American actress

James Woods, American actor

        Gerry Rafferty, British singer/songwriter

Iggy Pop, American singer/songwriter

        Elton John, British singer/songwriter

Lesley Collier, British ballerina

        Ry Cooder, American musician

Billy Crystal, American actor

        Glenn Close, American actress

Carol Bayer Sager, American songwriter

    Jennifer Warnes, American singer

Shakira Caine, Guyanan-born model and wife of Michael Caine

    Rupert Holmes, American singer/songwriter, composer and novelist

Edward James Olmos, American actor

    Stephanie Beacham, British actress

Kiki Dee, British singer

    Rob Reiner, American film director and actor

Dick Fosbury, American athlete

Melanie, American singer

Farrah Fawcett, American actress

Dave Davies, British musician

Dan Quayle, American vice president

José María Canizares, Spanish golfer

Peter Strauss, American actor

Jill Eikenberry, American actress

David Bowie, British musician

Would Have Turned 60 in 2007

Marc Bolan, British singer/songwriter

Sandy Denny, British singer

Steve Marriott, British singer

Laura Nyro, American singer/songwriter

Tim Buckley, American singer/songwriter

Mickey Finn, British musician

Kathy Acker, American writer

James Hunt, British racing driver

Minnie Ripperton, American singer

Pete Ham, British musician

Cozy Powell, British musician

Warren Zevon, American singer/songwriter

Turn 50 in 2007

Shane MacGowan, British musician

Steve Buscemi, American actor

Anita Baker, American singer and composer

Anita Ward, American singer

Ray Romano, American actor and comedian

Caroline Kennedy, daughter of American president JFK

Donny Osmond, American singer

Michael McShane, American actor

Nancy Cartwright, American actress

Lyle Lovett, American singer/songwriter

Dolph Lundgren, Swedish actor

Lori Singer, American actress

Gloria Estefan, American singer

Ethan Coen, American director

Melanie Griffith, American actress

Carole Bouquet, French actress

Denis Leary, American actor

Kim Sledge, American singer

Stephen Fry, British writer, actor and comedian

Bernhard Langer, German golfer

Daniel Stern, American actor

Nick Faldo, British golfer

Kate Buffery, British actress

Wayne Grady, Australian golfer

Timothy Busfield, American actor

Frances McDormand, American actress

Kelly McGillis, American actress

Cameron Crowe, American film director

Richard E. Grant, British actor

Peter Howitt, British actor and director

Judge Reinhold, American actor

Severiano Ballesteros, Spanish golfer

Vince Gill, American singer/songwriter

Robert Harris, British writer

Daniel Day-Lewis, British actor

Spike Lee, American film director

Theresa Russell, American actress

Stephanie Mills, American actress and singer

Amanda Plummer, American actress

Leeza Gibbons, American TV host

Marlon Jackson, American singer

Christopher Lambert, French actor

Paul Reiser, American actor and comedian

Timothy Spall, British actor

Marita Koch, German athlete

Vanna White, American game-show star

Ray Winstone, British actor

John Turturro, American actor

Cindy Wilson, American musician

Mario Van Peebles, American film director

Princess Caroline of Monaco

Adrian Edmondson, British comedian

Nick Price, Rhodesian golfer

Nancy Lopez, American golfer

Katie Couric, American TV host

Mark O'Meara, American golfer

Would Have Turned 50 in 2007

Payne Stewart, American golfer

Falco, Austrian singer

Sid Vicious, British musician

Laura Branigan, American singer

Turn 40 in 2007

Boris Becker, German tennis player

Anna Nicole Smith, American model

Donovan Bailey, Canadian athlete

Jamie Foxx, American actor and comedian

Amy Carter, daughter of American president Jimmy Carter

Monica Ali, British novelist

Lisa Bonet, American actress

Julia Roberts, American actress

Kevin Macdonald, British film director

Rufus Sewell, British actor

Gavin Rossdale, British singer/songwriter

Courtney Thorne-Smith, American actress

Donya Fiorentino, American model

Tara Fitzgerald, British actress

Faith Hill, American singer

Mira Sorvino, American actress

Moon Unit Zappa, American singer

Brett Anderson, British rock singer

Andrea Roth, Canadian actress

Thomas Muster, Austrian tennis player

Frankie Fredericks, Namibian athlete

Toni Braxton, American singer

Aaron Krickstein, South African tennis player

Charlotte Lewis, British actress

Quinn Cummings, American actress

Harry Connick Jr., American singer and actor

Michael Johnson, American athlete

Pamela Anderson, Canadian model and actress

Will Ferrell, American comedian and actor

287

Vin Diesel, American actor, writer and director

Philip Seymour Hoffman, American actor

Matt LeBlanc, American actor

Noel Gallagher, British singer/songwriter

Mia Sara, American actress

Sadie Frost, British actress

Sherry Stringfield, American actress

Nicole Kidman, Australian actress

Kathy Rinaldi, American tennis player

Melina Kanakaredes, American actress

Marianne Jean-Baptiste, British actress and composer

Kari Wuhrer, American singer and MTV DJ

Apache Indian, British rapper

Heinz-Harald Frentzen, German racing driver

Phil Selway, British musician

Billy Corgan, American musician

Tia Carrere, American actress

Vendela, Swedish model

Emily Watson, British actress

Laura Dern, American actress

Benicio Del Toro, Puerto Rican actor

Andrew Shue, American actor

Turn 30 in 2007

James Blunt, British singer/songwriter

Orlando Bloom, British actor

Joey Fatone, American singer

Shakira, Colombian singer

Chris Martin, British musician

Ronan Keating, Irish singer

James Van Der Beek, American actor

Sarah Michelle Gellar, American actress

Ben Curtis, American golfer

Samantha Morton, British actress

Liv Tyler, American actress

Jonathan Rhys-Meyers, Irish actor

Fiona Apple, American singer/songwriter

Sophie Dahl, British supermodel

Brittany Murphy, American actress

Colin Hanks, American actor

Peter Phillips, British royal

Bridget Hall, American model

289

Turn 25 in 2007

Prince William, British royal

Anna Paquin, Canadian actress

LeAnn Rimes, American singer

Andy Roddick, American tennis player

Kelly Clarkson, American singer

Kirsten Dunst, American actress

Justine Henin-Hardene, Belgian tennis player

Tara Lipinski, American ice-skater

Leelee Sobieski, American actress

David Nalbandian, Argentinean tennis player

Jessica Biel, American actress

Kieran Culkin, American actor

Ian Thorpe, Australian swimmer

Turn 21 in 2007

Charlotte Church, British singer

Jamie Bell, British actor

Mary-Kate and Ashley Olsen, American actresses and entrepreneurs

Lindsay Lohan, American actress

Amir Khan, British boxer

Turn 20 in 2007

Hilary Duff, American actress and singer

Aaron Carter, American actor and singer

Joss Stone, British singer/songwriter

Maria Sharapova, Russian tennis star

Andrew Murray, British tennis player

Katy Rose, American singer

What People Did in World War II

Jack Palance was a pilot and was shot down—sustaining severe facial burns resulting in major plastic surgery. He was awarded the Purple Heart.

Eli Wallach served in the U.S. Army Medical Corps and helped treat casualties in Europe.

Peter Sellers was in the Entertainments Division of the RAF and was attached to the Ralph Reader Gang Show.

Leslie Nielsen joined the Royal Canadian Air Force and trained as an air gunner, but the war ended before he could see combat.

David Tomlinson (Mr. Banks in *Mary Poppins*) served as a flight lieutenant in the RAF.

Aaron Spelling served in the U.S. Army Air Force and was awarded the Bronze Star and Purple Heart with Oak Leaf Cluster.

Edward Heath served in the Royal Artillery, rising to the rank of major and getting a mention in dispatches as well as being awarded a military Member of the Order of the British Empire.

Bill Travers was sent to India's Northwest Frontier to join a Gurkha regiment that was operating behind enemy lines alongside General Wingate's Chindits. He parachuted into the Malayan jungle in command of a small group of men to harass the Japanese.

Ian Carmichael served as a major in the 22 Dragoons in northwest Europe, gaining a mention in dispatches.

Telly Savalas served with the U.S. Army toward the end of the war and was injured in action.

Rossano Brazzi joined the Italian Resistance after his parents were murdered by the Fascists. He also continued to make films during the war.

Dinah Shore traveled more miles than any other American entertainer to entertain the troops.

Jeff Chandler served in the army in the Pacific, rising from infantryman to first lieutenant.

President George Bush was the U.S. Navy's youngest ever fighter pilot. He flew fifty-eight missions and was once shot down (and rescued). He won five medals.

Prince Philip served in the Royal Navy and captained a ship.

Lorne Greene served in the Royal Canadian Air Force.

Martin Balsam served in the U.S. Army Combat Engineers before transferring to the U.S. Army Air Force.

George MacDonald Fraser served in the British army in Burma.

Robert Altman was a bomber pilot in the Pacific.

Johnny Carson served with the U.S. Naval Reserve.

Things Said by Winston Churchill

"I have never accepted what many people have kindly said, namely that I inspired the nation. It was the nation and the race dwelling all round the globe that had the lion heart. I had the luck to be called upon to give the roar."

Anonymous Labor MP: "Must you fall asleep while I am speaking?"

Winston Churchill: "No, it is purely voluntary."

Bessie Braddock: "Winston, you're drunk!"
Winston Churchill: "Bessie, you're ugly. But tomorrow morning I shall be sober."

George Bernard Shaw: "Am reserving two tickets for you for my premiere. Come and bring a friend—if you have one."
Winston Churchill: "Impossible to be present for the first performance. Will attend the second—if there is one."

"We are all worms, but I do believe that I am a glowworm."

"When I look back on all the worries, I remember the story of the old man who said on his deathbed that he had a lot of trouble in his life, most of which never happened."

"Solitary trees, if they grow at all, grow strong."

"Men stumble over the truth from time to time, but most pick themselves up and hurry off as if nothing happened."

"History will be kind to me, for I intend to write it."

"In my belief, you cannot deal with the most serious things in the world unless you also understand the most amusing."

"We make a living by what we get. We make a life by what we give."

"I am ready to meet my Maker. Whether my Maker is prepared for the great ordeal of meeting me is another matter."

Sports

Jennifer Lopez was a star high school gymnast.

Jason Statham was a diver who represented Great Britain in the Seoul Olympics.

Kate Bosworth was a champion equestrian and played varsity soccer and lacrosse.

Joely Richardson attended a Florida tennis academy for two years.

50 Cent was a talented boxer who nurtured ambitions to turn professional.

A baseball hit by a bat travels as fast as 120 miles per hour—almost precisely the same (maximum) speed as the puck in ice hockey.

Keira Knightley, Madonna and Uma Thurman are all avid fencers.

There are 108 stitches on a baseball.

Australian Rules Football was originally designed to give crick-eters something to play during the off-season.

Johnny Mathis has scored a hole in one on no fewer than five occasions.

Arthur Conan Doyle was an avid amateur cricketer who bowled the great W. G. Grace in 1900.

Lord Byron was an all-around sportsman who captained Harrow in their annual cricket match against Eton at Lord's.

It takes 3,000 cows to supply the U.S. National Football League (NFL) with enough leather for a year's supply of footballs.

Eminem is an avid darts player.

The average life span of a major-league baseball is seven pitches.

A Costa Rican worker making baseballs earns around $3,000 per annum. The average American pro baseball player earns around $2.5 million per annum.

The bull's-eye on a dartboard must be precisely 5 feet 8 inches off the ground.

There are two sports in which the team has to move backward to win: tug-of-war and rowing. (N.B.: Backstroke is not a team sport.)

In 1972, an entire soccer team in Córdoba, Argentina, was jailed after the players kicked a linesman to death.

Eddie Arcaro won nearly 5,000 races to be ranked one of the greatest jockeys of all time, but, incredibly, he rode 250 losers before he won his first race.

Babe Ruth wore a cabbage leaf under his baseball cap to keep him cool.

When volleyball was first invented in 1895, it was called mintonette.

People Who've Run Marathons

Jeffrey Archer (London)

Sean "P. Diddy" Combs (New York City)

Will Ferrell (Boston)

Jorg Haider (New York City)

Oprah Winfrey (Marine Corps)

Avid Squash Players

Tom Cruise, Michael Palin, Nicole Kidman, Ian McShane, Damon Hill

Avid Tennis Players

Robert Duvall, Tony Blair, Martin Amis, David Frost, Richard Branson, James Fox, Jung Chang, Jackie Stewart, Michelle Trachtenberg

Fond of Sailing

John Major, Jeremy Irons, Elle MacPherson, Kelsey Grammer, Chloe Sevigny, Russell Crowe

Avid Table-Tennis Players

Kevin Spacey (requests a Ping-Pong table in his room whenever he's on location), Matthew Broderick

Women Who are Avid Golfers

Catherine Zeta-Jones, Claudia Schiffer, Teri Hatcher, Céline Dion, Cindy Crawford, Nicole Kidman, Michelle Trachtenberg

Avid Snooker (etc.) Players

Noah Wyle (plays billiards like a pool shark at the Hollywood Athletic Club), Kelsey Grammer (billiards), Finley Quaye (was a snooker hustler as a boy), Lisa Kudrow (plays pool like a pool shark and can perform trick shots)

The Seven Deadly Sins

Anger, avarice, envy, gluttony, lust, pride and sloth

The Seven Virtues

Charity, courage, faith, hope, justice, prudence and temperance

If . . .

If Holly Hunter married George W. Bush, she'd be Holly Bush.

If Iman married Gary Oldman, she'd be Iman Oldman.

If Cherie Blair married Oliver Stone, she'd be Cherie Stone.

If Olivia Newton-John married Wayne Newton, then divorced him to marry Elton John, she'd be Olivia Newton-John Newton John.

James Bond

"Who was the first person to play James Bond?" is a famous trick question. No, it wasn't Sean Connery, even though he was the first *movie* James Bond (in *Dr. No*). In 1954, James Bond was played by Barry Nelson in a one-hour U.S. TV version of *Casino Royale*. Le Chiffre, the baddie, was played by Peter Lorre.

Since Barry Nelson, Bond has been played by Connery, George Lazenby, Roger Moore, Timothy Dalton and Pierce Brosnan (as well as by David Niven in the spoof *Casino Royale*).

Ian Fleming, the creator of Bond, took his hero's name from an ornithologist. Fleming was a keen bird-watcher, and when he was looking for a name, he picked up a book by a distinguished American ornithologist named James Bond and decided to "borrow" it.

He also "borrowed" the name of Bond's greatest enemy, Blofeld. Fleming had been pondering over a suitably nasty name for his villain when he chanced upon the name of Henry Blofeld, now a cricket commentator, in Boodles, the London gentlemen's club.

James Bond is renowned for his smooth talking. In *Diamonds Are Forever*, when Tiffany Case (Jill St. John) asks him, "Do you like redheads?" he replies, "As long as the collars and cuffs match."

For most people Sean Connery *is* Bond, but Connery himself described the character as "a Frankenstein monster I can't get rid of" and has said, "I have always hated that damn James Bond: I'd like to kill him."

James Bond has been going for so long that *Goldeneye* saw the first appearance by the *daughter* of a Bond girl. Eunice Grayson appeared in the first two Bond movies (indeed, it was to her that Bond first uttered the immortal words, "The name's Bond, James Bond") and her daughter, Karen, age 24, appeared in *Goldeneye*.

Bond's cars are almost as essential to the films' successes as the villains and the girls. His most famous car is the Aston Martin DB5 with revolving license plates, pop-up bulletproof shield and ejector seat that he drove in *Goldfinger*.

But if *Goldfinger* had the most memorable car, *Diamonds Are Forever* had the most memorable car stunt. That was the film when Connery (or his stuntman) two-wheeled a Ford Mustang down a narrow alleyway and then set it back on four wheels.

Bond Films and Their Titles Overseas (translated back into English)

Dr. No: *License to Kill* (Italy)

From Russia with Love: *Agent 007 Sees Red* (Sweden)

Thunderball: *Agent 007 into the Fire* (Denmark)

You Only Live Twice: *007 Dies Twice* (Japan)

Live and Let Die: *The Dead Slave (Japan)*

For Your Eyes Only: *A Deadly Mission* (Germany)

Octopussy: *Operation Octopus* (Italy)

A View to a Kill: *Dangerously Yours* (France)

The Living Daylights: *Death Is Not a Game* (Belgium)

License to Kill: *Private Revenge* (Italy)

Other People Born on Christmas Day

1642 Isaac Newton, English scientist

1899 Humphrey Bogart, American actor

1901 Princess Alice, British royal

1907 Cab Calloway, American musician

1908 Quentin Crisp, British writer and personality

1912 Tony Martin, American actor and singer

1918 Anwar Sadat, Egyptian politician

1923 Noele Gordon, British actress

1924 Rod Serling, American writer

1927 Alan King, American comedian

1936 Princess Alexandra, British royal

1936 Ismail Merchant, Indian film producer

1937 O'Kelly Isley, American singer

1943 Hanna Schygulla, German actress

1945 Noel Redding, British musician (in the Jimi Hendrix Experience)

1946 Jimmy Buffett, American singer

1948 Merry Clayton, American singer

1948 Barbara Mandrell, American singer

1949 Sissy Spacek, American actress

1954 Robin Campbell, British musician

1954 Annie Lennox, British singer

1957 Shane MacGowan, British musician

1968 Helena Christensen, Danish model

1971 Dido, British singer

Things Said About Christmas

"Next to a circus there ain't nothing that packs up and tears out faster than the Christmas spirit." (Kin Hubbard)

"Christmas is a holiday that persecutes the lonely, the frayed, and the rejected." (Jimmy Cannon)

"What is Christmas? It is tenderness for the past, courage for the present, hope for the future. It is a fervent wish that every cup may overflow with blessings rich and eternal, and that every path may lead to peace." (Agnes Pharo)

"**There is no** ideal Christmas; only the one Christmas you decide to make as a reflection of your values, desires, affections, traditions." (Bill McKibben)

"**Christmas waves** a magic wand over this world, and behold, everything is softer and more beautiful." (Norman Vincent Peale)

"**Blessed is** the season which engages the whole world in a conspiracy of love." (Hamilton Wright Mabie)

"**Christmas, children,** is not a date. It is a state of mind." (Mary Ellen Chase)

Genuine Place-Names, for Lovers of Double Entendre

Arsy (France)

Bald Knob (Arkansas)

Balls Cross (West Sussex, U.K.)

Bastardo (Italy)

Beaver (Pennsylvania)

Bendery (Moldova)

Big Bone Lick (Kentucky)

Blowing Rock (North Carolina)

Bottom (North Carolina)

Bra (Italy)

Broadbottom (Greater Manchester, U.K.)

Burrumbuttock (Australia)

Buttock's Booth (Northamptonshire, U.K.)

Climax (Michigan)

Clit (Romania)

Cock Bank (Clwyd, U.K.)

Cockermouth (Cumbria, U.K.)

Comers (Grampian, U.K.)

Condom (France)

Dildo (Canada)

Fertile (Minnesota)

French Lick (Indiana)

Fucking (Austria)

Hornytown (North Carolina)

Humptulips (Washington)

Intercourse (Pennsylvania)

Knob Lick (Missouri)

Knockin (Shropshire, U.K.)

Lickey End (Worcestershire, U.K.)

Loveladies (New Jersey)

Lover (Wiltshire, U.K.)

Muff (Northern Ireland)

Neck City (Missouri)

Penistone (South Yorkshire, U.K.)

Petting (Germany)

Phuket (Thailand)

Root (Switzerland)

Semen (Indonesia)

Shafton (Yorkshire, U.K.)

Shag Harbour (Canada)

Thong (Kent, U.K.)

Titz (Germany)

Twatt (Orkney, U.K.)

Twin Humps Park (Australia)

Undy (Gwent, U.K.)

Upper Dicker (East Sussex, U.K.)

Wankers Corner (Oregon)

Wide Open (Tyne and Wear, U.K.)

Marriage, Etc.

Four of Mickey Rooney's weddings took place in Las Vegas.

Woody Harrelson married Neil Simon's daughter.

Ruth Rendell, Art Carney and Alexander Solzhenitsyn all remarried their spouses after divorce.

Sheryl Lee married Neil Diamond's son.

Couples Who Celebrated Their Diamond Wedding Anniversary

Perry and Roselle Como

Bob and Dolores Hope

James and Frances Cagney

Alec and Merula Guinness

Karl and Mona Malden

Former British prime minister James and Audrey Callaghan

Fred Zinnemann and Renee Bartlett

John Mills and Mary Hayley Bell

Richard Attenborough and Sheila Sim

George and Barbara Bush

Charlton and Lydia Heston

Couples Who Celebrated Their Golden Wedding Anniversary

Catherine and Tom Cookson

Jack and Florence Haley

Ray and Gwendolyn Bolger

Walter and Ruth Pidgeon

Hume Cronyn and Jessica Tandy

Pat and Eloise O'Brien

Carl and Emma Jung

Queen Elizabeth II and Prince Philip

Dick and Mary Francis

Yehudi and Diana Menuhin

Googie Withers and John McCallum

Federico Fellini and Giulietta Masina

Marlene Dietrich and Rudolf Sieber

Eli and Anne Wallach

People Who Were/Are Married to Their Manager

Neneh Cherry, Joe Bugner, Céline Dion, Charlotte Rampling, LaToya Jackson, Judy Garland, Randy Travis, 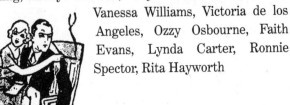 Vanessa Williams, Victoria de los Angeles, Ozzy Osbourne, Faith Evans, Lynda Carter, Ronnie Spector, Rita Hayworth

People Who Married Their Bodyguard

Roseanne Arnold, Patty Hearst, Princess Stephanie of Monaco

People with Spouses in Common

Sonny Bono and Gregg Allman—Cher

Peter Sellers and Slim Jim McDonnell—Britt Ekland

Dudley Moore and Pinchas Zukerman—Tuesday Weld

Gary Kemp and Jude Law—Sadie Frost

Mia Farrow and Ava Gardner—Frank Sinatra

Henry Fonda and William Wyler—Margaret Sullavan

Rex Harrison and Richard Harris—Elizabeth Harris

Artie Shaw and Lex Barker—Lana Turner

Humphrey Bogart and Jason Robards—Lauren Bacall

Mimi Rogers and Nicole Kidman—Tom Cruise

Ursula Andress and Linda Evans—John Derek

Vivien Leigh and Joan Plowright—Laurence Olivier

Brigitte Bardot and Jane Fonda—Roger Vadim

Peter Sellers and David Frost—Lynne Frederick

Charlie Chaplin and Burgess Meredith—Paulette Goddard

George Sanders and Ronald Colman—Benita Hume

Laurence Harvey and Michael Wilding—Margaret Leighton

Clark Gable and William Powell—Carole Lombard

Germaine Greer and Maya Angelou—Paul de Feu

Franchot Tone and Douglas Fairbanks Jr.—Joan Crawford

Don Johnson and Antonio Banderas—Melanie Griffith

Elizabeth Taylor and Joan Blondell—Mike Todd

Elizabeth Taylor and Debbie Reynolds—Eddie Fisher

Rod Steiger and Philip Roth—Claire Bloom

Roger Vadim and Ted Turner—Jane Fonda

Gloria Swanson and Constance Bennett—Marquis de la Coudraye

Myrna Loy and Hedy Lamarr—Gene Markey

Lana Turner and Arlene Dahl—Lex Barker

Nancy Reagan and Jane Wyman—Ronald Reagan

Lana Turner and Evelyn Keyes—Artie Shaw

Mickey Rooney and Artie Shaw—Ava Gardner

John Huston and Artie Shaw—Evelyn Keyes

Gene Tierney and Hedy Lamarr—Howard Lee

Joan Fontaine and Ida Lupino—Collier Young

Joe DiMaggio and Arthur Miller—Marilyn Monroe

Jeanne Moreau and Lesley-Anne Down—William Friedkin

John F. Kennedy and Aristotle Onassis—Jacqueline Onassis

Rachel Roberts and Kay Kendall—Rex Harrison

Jennie Churchill and Mrs. Patrick Campbell—George Cornwallis-West

Stavros Niarchos and Aristotle Onassis—Tina Livanos

James Hunt and Richard Burton—Suzy Hunt

Paulette Goddard and Oona O'Neill—Charlie Chaplin

People Who Never Married

Julie Christie, Cliff Richard, Ralph Nader, Leonard Cohen

Things That Simply Disappeared

Pet Rocks

Clackers

Hairstyles such as the Elephant's Trunk, Argentine Ducktail, Flattop, Conk, Spike Top, Suedehead and Flop

Things Said About Growing Old

"Anyone can get old. All you have to do is live long enough." (Groucho Marx)

> **"It doesn't matter** how many face lifts you have. You can't fool two flights of stairs." (Max Bygraves)

"To me, old age is always fifteen years older than I am." (Bernard M. Baruch)

> **"As we grow** old . . . the beauty steals inward." (Ralph Waldo Emerson)

"The great secret that all old people share is that you really haven't changed in seventy or eighty years. Your body changes, but you don't change at all." (Doris Lessing)

> **"The longer I** live, the more beautiful life becomes." (Frank Lloyd Wright)

"You're never too old to become younger." (Mae West)

> **"It is a mistake** to regard age as a downhill grade toward dissolution. The reverse is true. As one grows older, one climbs with surprising strides." (George Sand)

"The secret of staying young is to live honestly, eat slowly, and lie about your age." (Lucille Ball)

> **"Old age is** not so bad when you consider the alternatives." (Maurice Chevalier)

"To be seventy years young is sometimes far more cheerful and hopeful than to be forty years old." (Oliver Wendell Holmes)

> **"No matter how** old you are, there's always something good to look forward to." (Lynn Johnston)

"You can only perceive real beauty in a person as they get older." (Anouk Aimée)

> **"We did not** change as we grew older; we just became more clearly ourselves." (Lynn Hall)

"The older I grow, the more I distrust the familiar doctrine that age brings wisdom." (H. L. Mencken)

> **"You know you're** getting old when the candles cost more than the cake." (Bob Hope)

Women Who Died in Childbirth

Jane Seymour (third wife of Henry VIII, while giving birth to future Edward VI)

> **Two of** Joseph Chamberlain's wives (one of whom was Neville Chamberlain's mother, who died when he was six)

James Watt's wife

> **Mary Shelley's** mother (Mary Wollstonecraft)

John Donne's wife

Charles Babbage's wife

Kenneth Grahame's mother (when he was five)

Princess Charlotte

Haing Ngor's wife (the Khmer Rouge's hatred of professionals meant he was unable to reveal that he was a gynecologist and needed medical supplies to help her)

Al Jolson's mother (when he was eight)

Walter Pidgeon's first wife

Franz Liszt's daughter

Robert Johnson's first wife (age sixteen)

Three of Jane Austen's sisters-in-law

Kim Il-sung's first wife

Emperor Haile Selassie's daughter

Catherine Parr (sixth wife of Henry VIII)

Men Whose Penis Was Preserved After Death

Napoleon Bonaparte (It was eventually sold at auction, where it fetched £2,500.)

Grigory Rasputin (According to his biographer, "It looked like a blackened overripe banana, about a foot long. . . .")

People Who Died of Lung Cancer

Steve McQueen, Jacques Brel, Yul Brynner, Joe DiMaggio, John Wayne, Buddy Adler, Duke Ellington, Roddy McDowall, Stubby Kaye, Buster Keaton, Desi Arnaz, Tex Avery, Bruce Cabot, Art Blakey, Cantinflas, King George VI, Lon Chaney, Andy Kaufman, Chuck Connors, Frank Loesser, E. G. Marshall, Franchot Tone, Gary Cooper, Walt Disney, Dick Haymes, Harry Guardino, Moe Howard, Eddie Kendricks, Warren Zevon, Doug McClure, Ray Milland, Robert Mitchum, Forrest Tucker, Boris Pasternak, Lloyd Nolan, Jesse Owens, Robert Preston, Carl Wilson, Vincent Price, Eddie Rabbitt, Alan Jay Lerner, Nicholas Ray, Robert Taylor, Stanley Baker, Gilbert Becaud, Nat "King" Cole, Albert Collins, Rosemary Clooney, Betty Grable, Melina Mercouri, Agnes Moorehead, Jacqueline Susann, Sarah Vaughan, Nancy Walker

Celebrity Bequests

Two days before her death in 1970, Janis Joplin amended her will to provide $2,500 "so my friends can get blasted after I'm gone." She also left a guest list. The all-night party duly took place at a Californian tavern where she had often performed.

In 1964, Ian Fleming, the author of the James Bond novels, left £500 to each of four friends with the instruction that they should "spend the same within twelve months of receipt on some extravagance."

In 1962, Marilyn Monroe left all her "personal effects and clothing" to Lee Strasberg, her acting coach, "it being my desire that he distribute these, in his sole discretion, among my friends, colleagues and those to whom I am devoted." She also left Strasberg most of her estate.

In 1986, Cary Grant bequeathed all of his "wearing apparel, ornaments and jewelry" to Stanley E. Fox on condition that Mr. Fox shared everything out among 14 specified people—one of whom was Frank Sinatra.

W. C. Fields's last requests, as listed in his will, were ignored. He wanted his body cremated without any religious ceremony. However, both his estranged Roman Catholic wife and his mistress held separate religious ceremonies before his body was interred in a mausoleum in 1946. Nor did anything come of the provision he had made for a "W. C. Fields College for orphan white boys and girls where no religion of any sort is to be preached."

P. T. Barnum, the famous American showman, drew up a will in 1882 leaving his daughter Helen $1,500 a year for life. When she left her husband, Barnum wrote her out of the will. Then, in an 1889 codicil, he left her a property in Colorado, which he believed was worthless. Two years later he died, and Helen inherited this property, which turned out to have mineral deposits that made Helen wealthier than all the other beneficiaries of Barnum's will combined.

In 1964, Cole Porter bequeathed his diamond dress stud to Douglas Fairbanks Jr.

In his will, Noah gave the whole world to his three sons.

Pairs of Famous People Who Died on the Same Day

John Adams (second U.S. President) and Thomas Jefferson (third U.S. President)—July 4, 1826

Charles Kingsley (author of *The Water Babies*) and Gustave Doré (painter)—January 23, 1883

Franz Liszt (classical composer) and Frank Holl (painter)—July 31, 1888

Wilkie Collins (novelist) and Eliza Cook (poet)—
September 23, 1889

John Ruskin (social reformer, artist and writer) and Richard Doddridge Blackmore (author of *Lorna Doone*)—January 20, 1900

Carl Bechstein (maker of the famous Bechstein pianos) and Gottlieb Daimler (automobile manufacturer)—
March 6, 1900

Marshal Henri Pétain (French soldier and leader of the wartime Vichy regime) and Robert Flaherty (filmmaker and explorer)—July 23, 1951

Josef Stalin (Soviet dictator) and Sergei Prokofiev (composer who was persecuted by Stalin)—March 5, 1953

King Ibn Saud (of Saudi Arabia) and Dylan Thomas (poet)—November 9, 1953

Ward Bond (actor) and Mack Sennett (film producer)—November 5, 1960

Michael Curtiz (film director) and Stu Sutcliffe (former member of the Beatles)—October 10, 1962

Jean Cocteau (playwright and film director) and Edith Piaf (singer)—October 11, 1963

Hedda Hopper (gossip columnist) and Buster Keaton (actor)—February 1, 1966

Billy Rose (Broadway producer) and Sophie Tucker (singer)—February 10, 1966

Che Guevara (revolutionary) and André Maurois (French author)—October 9, 1967

> **Mama Cass Elliot** (singer) and Erich Kästner (author of *Emil and the Detectives*)—July 29, 1974

Steve Biko (antiapartheid activist) and Robert Lowell (American poet)—September 12, 1977

> **Joyce Grenfell** (actress and writer) and Zeppo Marx (member of the Marx Brothers)—November 30, 1979

Thelonious Monk (jazz musician) and Lee Strasberg (actor and drama teacher)—February 17, 1982

> **Muddy Waters** (blues musician) and George Balanchine (choreographer)—April 30, 1983

William Powell (film star) and Tito Gobbi (opera singer)—March 5, 1984

> **Carl Foreman** (film producer) and George Gallup (pollster)—June 26, 1984

Sam Spiegel (film producer) and Ricky Nelson (pop star)—December 31, 1985

> **Gordon Macrae** (actor), L. Ron Hubbard (creator of Scientology) and Vincente Minnelli (film director)—January 24, 1986

Alan Jay Lerner (lyricist) and Jorge Luis Borges (writer)—June 14, 1986

> **Randolph Scott** (actor) and Joan Greenwood (actress)—March 2, 1987

Mary Astor (actress) and Emlyn Williams (actor and playwright)—September 25, 1987

Sugar Ray Robinson (boxer) and Abbie Hoffman (political activist and writer)—April 12, 1989

George Adamson (*Born Free* conservationist) and Diana Vreeland (fashion guru)—August 21, 1989

Steve Marriott (rock star) and Don Siegel (film director)—April 20, 1991

Stella Adler (drama teacher) and Albert King (blues singer)—December 21, 1992

James Hunt (racing driver) and John Connally (former Texas governor and U.S. presidential candidate, who was shot while riding in the same car as President Kennedy when he was assassinated)—June 15, 1993

Elizabeth Montgomery (actress) and Elisha Cook Jr. (actor)—May 18, 1995

Mother Teresa (aid worker) and Georg Solti (orchestral conductor)—September 5, 1997

Carl Wilson (Beach Boy) and Falco (singer)—February 6, 1998

Bettino Craxi (Italian politician) and Hedy Lamarr (actress)—January 19, 2000

Charles M. Schulz (*Peanuts* creator) and Screamin' Jay Hawkins (blues legend)—February 12, 2000

John Gielgud (actor) and Barbara Cartland (writer)—
May 21, 2000

Perry Como (singer) and Didi (Brazilian footballer)—May 12, 2001

John Lee Hooker (blues legend) and Carroll O'Connor (actor)—June 21, 2001

Ken Tyrell (Formula 1 boss) and Aaliyah (singer)—August 25, 2001

Christiaan Barnard (heart-surgery pioneer) and Troy Donahue (actor)—September 2, 2001

Milton Berle (comedian) and Dudley Moore (actor and pianist)—March 27, 2002

Chaim Potok (writer) and Leo McKern (actor)—July 23, 2002

Paul Getty (philanthropist) and Dr. Robert Atkins (diet guru)—April 17, 2003

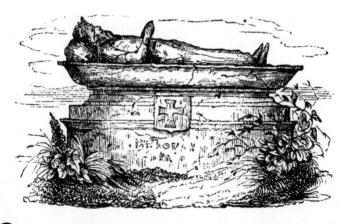

Robert Stack (actor) and Wendy Hiller (actress)—May 14, 2003

Strom Thurmond (U.S. senator) and Denis Thatcher (prime minister's husband)—June 26, 2003

Elia Kazan (film director) and Althea Gibson (tennis champion)—September 28, 2003

Alistair Cooke (broadcaster) and Hubert Gregg (performer and broadcaster)—March 30, 2004

Hunter S. Thompson (writer) and Sandra Dee (film star)—February 20, 2005

Edward Heath (British prime minister) and Geraldine Fitzgerald (actress)—July 17, 2005

People Who Died in Poverty

Josephine Baker, William Blake, Miguel de Cervantes, Christopher Columbus, Gustave Flaubert, Johann Gutenberg, Robert Johnson, Joe Louis, Herman Melville, Wolfgang Mozart, Thomas Paine, Edith Piaf, Rembrandt von Rijn, Oskar Schindler, Vincent van Gogh, Jan Vermeer, Oscar Wilde

People Who Were Murdered

Joe Orton (1967)

                  Ramon Novarro (1968)

Sharon Tate (1969)

                  Pier Paolo Pasolini (1975)

Sal Mineo (1976)

                  Bob Crane (1978)

Dorothy Stratten (1980)

                  Joy Adamson (1980)

John Lennon (1980)

                  Dominique Dunne (1982)

Felix Pappalardi (1983)

                  Dian Fossey (1985)

Andrés Escobar (1994)

                  Tupac Shakur (1996)

Haing S. Ngor (1996)

                  Veronica Guerin (1996)

Gianni Versace (1997)

                  Phil Hartman (1998)

Marie Trintignant (2003)

Famous People Born on the Day Other Famous People Died

David Schwimmer—November 2, 1966—Mississippi John Hurt

The Rock—May 2, 1972—J. Edgar Hoover

Pink—September 8, 1979—Jean Seberg

Sophie, Countess of Wessex—January 20, 1965—Alan Freed

Natalie Imbruglia—February 4, 1975—Louis Jordan

Divine Brown—August 9, 1969—Sharon Tate

Charlotte Rampling—February 5, 1946—George Arliss

Helena Sukova—February 23, 1965—Stan Laurel

Sinéad O'Connor—May 14, 1978—Robert Menzies

Ben Okri—March 15, 1959—Lester Young

Dennis Rodman—May 13, 1961—Gary Cooper

Mary-Kate and Ashley Olsen—June 13, 1986—Benny Goodman

Bill Withers—July 4, 1938—Suzanne Lenglen

Oscar de la Renta—July 22, 1932—Florenz Ziegfeld

Louise Fletcher –July 22, 1934—John Dillinger

Monica Lewinsky—July 23, 1973—Eddie Rickenbacker

Dino De Laurentiis—August 8, 1919—Frank Winfield Woolworth

Savo Milosevic—September 2, 1973—J. R. R. Tolkien

Holly Robinson—September 18, 1964—Sean O'Casey

Jenny McCarthy—November 1, 1972—Ezra Pound

Genuine IT Tech-Support Query

Customer: My keyboard is not working.

Tech-support: Are you sure it's plugged in to the computer?

Customer: No. I can't get behind the computer.

Tech-support: Pick up your keyboard and walk ten paces back.

Customer: Okay.

Tech-support: Did the keyboard come with you?

Customer: Yes.

Tech-support: That means the keyboard is not plugged in.

Lasts

The **last letter** George Harrison ever wrote was to Mike Myers asking for a Mini-Me doll.

11/19/1999 was the **last date** before 1/1/3111 when all the digits in the date were odd.

After **Custer's Last Stand,** Sioux Indian leader Chief Sitting Bull became an entertainer and toured the country with Buffalo Bill's Wild West Show.

The Beatles' last concert was in San Francisco in August 1966. (The **last song** in the concert was "Long Tall Sally.")

329

Elvis Presley's last concert was in Indianapolis in June 1977. (The **last song** in the concert was "Can't Help Falling in Love.")

The **last time** Olympic gold medals were made entirely from gold was 1912.

A **wooden racket** was **last used** at Wimbledon in 1987.

The **guillotine** was **last used** in France publicly in 1939 and nonpublicly in 1977.

The **last Civil War veteran** to die was John Salling, a Confederate soldier, who died in 1958 at age 112.

If a little knowledge is dangerous, where is
the man who has so much as to
be out of danger?
—*Thomas Huxley*

ACKNOWLEDGMENTS

The Other Book . . . of the Most Perfectly Useless Information is the third—and the last—in a series that started with *That Book . . . of Perfectly Useless Information* and continued with *This Book . . . of More Perfectly Useless Information*.

As with the first two books, most of *The Other Book* is the product of fascinating facts I've collected over the past twenty years and, therefore, unique to this book (or, rather, not *This Book* but *The Other Book*, if you get my drift). Nevertheless, as with the first two books, I am happy to acknowledge material culled from the Internet—especially in the sections on insects, the human condition, fish, geography, birds, history, animals and science—as well as fabulous contributions sent to me by friends and readers (sometimes by friends who are also readers or even by readers who have become friends).

As always, I welcome your e-mails—yup, even when you send corrections (how else will I ever get it right?)—so please contact me at: thatbook@mail.com

The Other Book was a team effort (even if I made damn sure that only my name appeared on the cover). So I'd like to thank: David Roth-Ey, Jeanette Perez, Maureen Sugden,

Doug Young, Mari Roberts, Penny Chorlton and Luigi Bonomi.

Since this is the last in the series, I'd also like to thank the following people for their help, contributions and/or support (moral or otherwise): Gilly Adams, Jeremy Beadle, Marcus Berkmann, Chris Ewins, Jonathan Fingerhut, Alan Fox, Jenny Garrison, Patrick Janson-Smith, Brian Johnson, Sam Jones, John Koski, Richard Littlejohn, Tricia Martin, William Mulcahy, Amanda Preston, Nicholas Ridge, Charlie Symons, Jack Symons, Louise Symons, Chris Tarrant, David Thomas and Rob Woolley.

As ever, if I've missed anyone, then please know that—as with any mistakes in the book—it's entirely down to my own stupidity.

LIST OF LISTS